Ex Libris
B212 © APCo

THE WORLD OF THE BIBLE

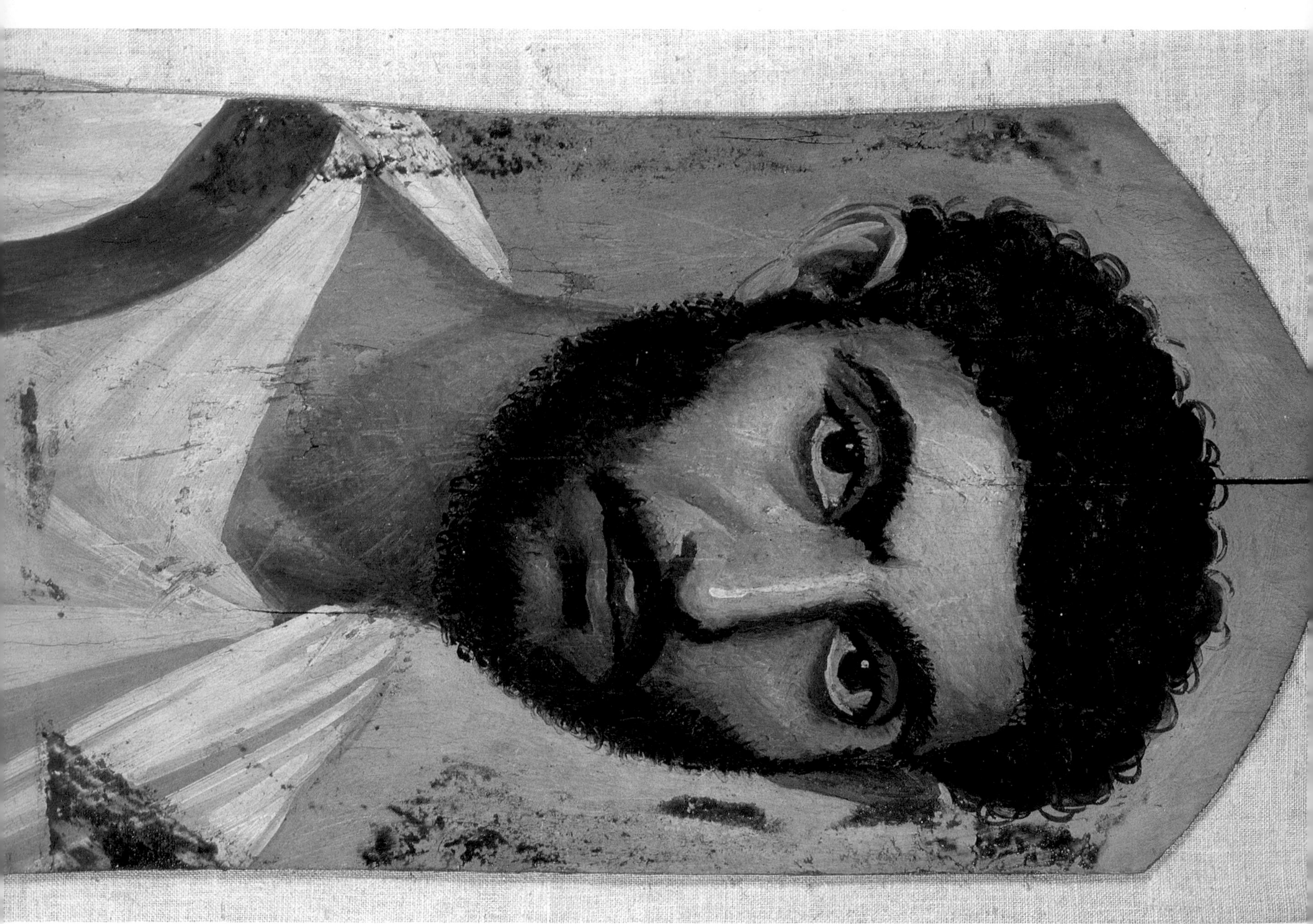

ROBERTA L. HARRIS

THE WORLD OF THE BIBLE

With 294 illustrations, 58 in color

THAMES AND HUDSON

For my parents, Rose and Maurice Harris and my husband, Jeremy, who have always helped and encouraged me.

Authors note
I could not have written this book without the support of my husband, Jeremy. My love and thanks go first to him – always. I should also like to acknowledge those friends and colleagues who have read the text of the book, and especially Shimon Gibson, whose advice prevented many errors. Such as are left are all my own. Many friends have allowed me to use their illustrative material, both photographs and drawings, and to them also go my thanks – to Hamam Habib Alwan, Professor Avraham Biran, Peter Bugod, Rupert Chapman, Professor Ehud Netzer, Esther Niv-Krendel, Dino Politis, Professor Avner Raban and Shelley Wachsmann. George Hart and Jonathan Tubb provided useful information. Eliot Braun in Israel gave me much practical advice and last, but not least, those staff at Thames and Hudson who waited so patiently for the book and whose professionalism has been a constant encouragement. They have also made the book a great deal of fun to work on.

Half-title: Bar Rekub of Zinjirli – a detail from his stela, dating to the second half of the 8th century BC*, now in the Pergamon Museum, Berlin.*
Title page: Fayuum portrait showing a Semitic type, dating to the Ptolemaic period, Egyptian Museum, Cairo.

First published in the United States of America in 1995 by Thames and Hudson Inc., 500 Fifth Avenue, New York, New York 10110

Library of Congress Catalog Card Number 94-60285

ISBN 0-500-05073-2

Printed and bound in Slovenia

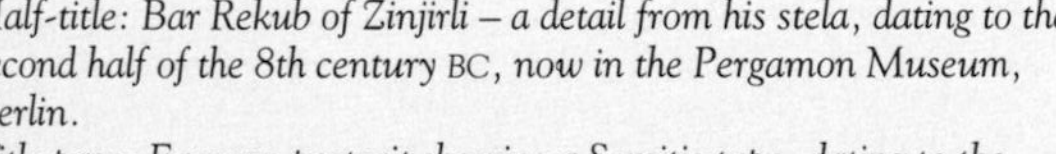

CONTENTS

IV
Widening Horizons

V
The Age of Jesus

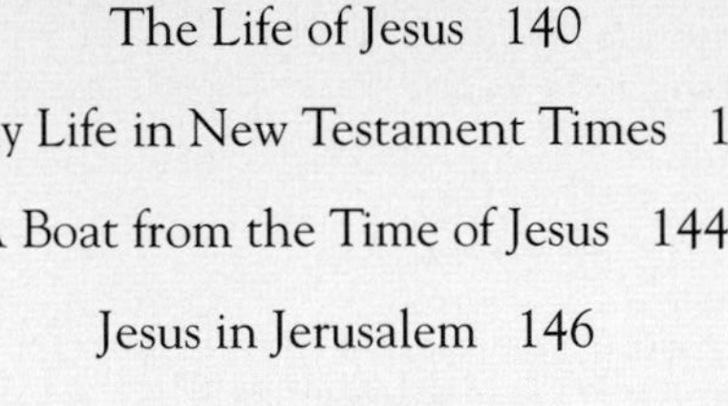

VI
The Turbulent Years

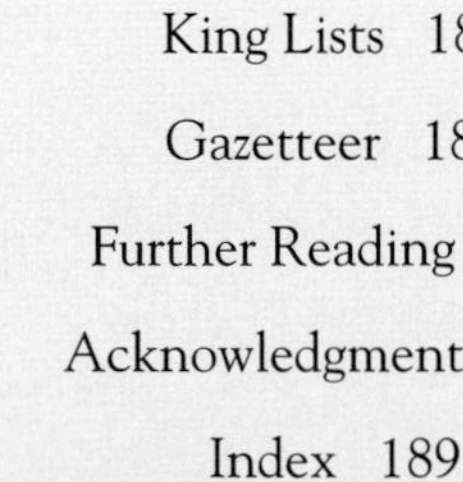

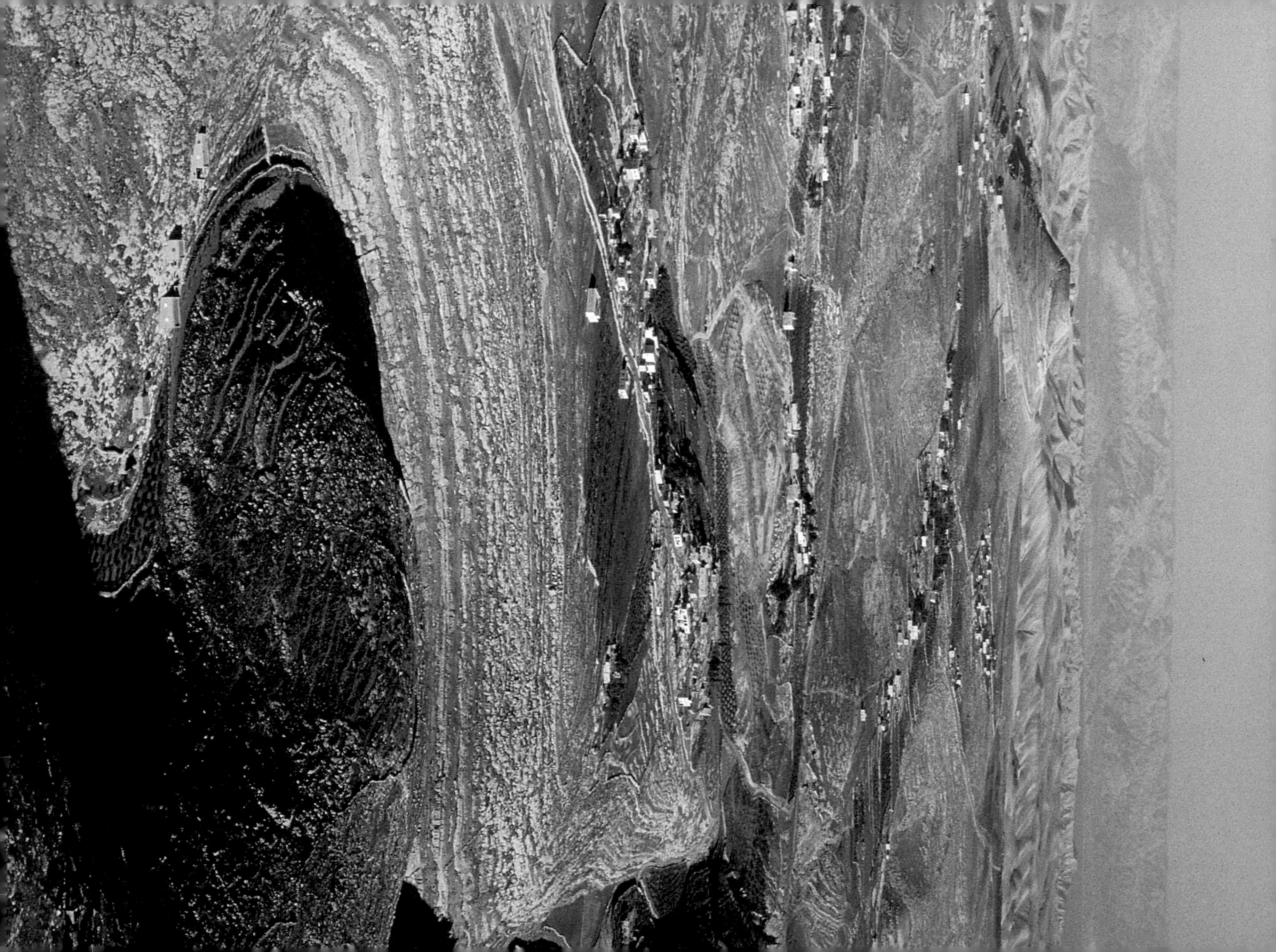

I

THE BIBLE IN CONTEXT

Unto thy seed will I give this land.
Genesis 12, 7

THE NEAR EAST has always been a region of extraordinary diversity of climate, terrain and cultures. The land of the Bible, tiny in itself and yet in some ways the pivot of the whole vast region, is a microcosm of that diversity. One indication of this is the many names by which the strip of land at the very eastern edge of the Mediterranean is known. To Jews, Christians and Moslems it is the Holy Land; to geographers it is the Levant; to archaeologists, Syro-Palestine; and to modern politicians it comprises the countries of Lebanon and Syria in the north, Israel and Jordan in the south. In ancient times this area was home to both the Israelites and the Canaanites, and, poor though it was, it gave the world two great treasures – the alphabet, and the Bible, which is the origin of and inspiration for three of the world's great religions.

This land has been fought over perhaps more than any other throughout history and possibly even before. In the days of the Bible, as empire succeeded empire, armies marched along the coastal strip, but few of the great kings of Assyria, Babylonia or Egypt thought it worth their while to campaign inland, into the hill country promised to Abraham and his descendants by God. It was never a rich or sophisticated place, and yet it was later conquered, reconquered and conquered again, by Romans, Moslems and Crusaders, to whom every inch of ground was holy. The arrival of European diplomats, missionaries, teachers and doctors in the 19th century marked renewed western interest in the Holy Land, though pilgrims and travellers, some intrepid women among them, had never ceased to visit. Later in the 19th century serious explorers came to map and measure the land scientifically. Then, from all over the world, came the archaeologists. Over the last century archaeology in the Holy Land has developed from a treasure hunt into an exacting and exciting discipline, although, even now, the work has only just begun.

A view of the Judaean Desert from the vicinity of Bethlehem. In the middle distance is Herodium, built by Herod the Great (p. 131). Beyond lies the Dead Sea, with the mountains of Jordan rising steeply on the other side.

GEOGRAPHY AND CLIMATE

Oases such as Jericho or Damascus attracted large numbers of people to settle at them, or to trade or simply to water their animals. Jericho was already a strongly fortified settlement in the late 9th millennium BC *(pp. 38–39), when few other places had large populations. In an arid land a reliable water supply is vital and friction between settled farmers and nomadic pastoralists often arose over access (Genesis 21, 25). However, other, more peaceful activities, such as the exchange of news and the arranging of marriages, also took place at oases, wells and springs (Genesis 24, 13–14; 29, 10–11).*

O Lord, how manifold are thy works! in wisdom hast thou made them all: the earth is full of thy riches.
Psalms 104, 24

THE AREA KNOWN AS THE NEAR (or Middle) East stretches from the Aegean coast of Asia Minor (that is, Anatolia or Turkey) in the west to the Persian plateau in the southeast, and from the Caucasus mountains and the Taurus/Zagros range in the north and northeast to the very tip of Arabia in the south. Egypt is also included, since that country has always been politically more a part of Asia than of Africa to which it geographically belongs. It is a huge landmass, and yet the areas in which people can live are very restricted. Mountain chains and high plateaux are too cold for human habitation and steppe and sand desert regions are too hot and arid.

People have always congregated in the great river valleys, such as the Tigris and Euphrates in Mesopotamia (this is now inland Syria and Iraq) or the Nile valley in Egypt. They also live along fertile coastal strips, like those of western Turkey, the Levant and southwest Arabia (Yemen), or they settle at oases, such as Damascus, Palmyra, Beersheba or Jericho. Since human beings are endlessly resourceful, at least one of the ancient civilizations of the Near East, the Hittite Empire, arose in the unlikely surroundings of the high steppes of central Anatolia, with its centre at Hattusas (today called Boghazköy). The greatest ancient civilizations of the region, however, arose in the river valleys of Mesopotamia and Egypt and were ultimately dependent on the techniques of irrigation agriculture.

The climate

Summers are hot and dry throughout the whole of the Near East. The coastal areas are a little cooler than the interior but the humidity is consequently greater. At high altitude summers can be pleasant, even a little cool at night, while the deserts daily reach temperatures of over 100 degrees F (38 degrees C). Nights in the desert usually feel chilly by comparison to the days. Winters can be very cold in the mountains or on high plateaux, such as Iran or inland Turkey. Jerusalem, at about 2,400 ft (730 m), may receive snowfall as late as April. Even the deserts of Arabia sometimes have snow, although it never lasts long. The coasts are not so cold, but are generally more rainy.

Water is easily the most valuable commodity in the region, so rainfall is very important in the places where groundwater resources are scarce. However, the rain is not very predictable from year to year. Wherever it does fall, the ground springs to life and is often thickly carpeted with flowers within days. This means that in the more marginal zones tribal herdsmen must be prepared to migrate frequently. Land which in some years would grow crops for a farmer, in others might only provide scrub grazing for herders. The constant shift in land use has often caused friction between agricultural communities and pastoralists in both ancient and modern times.

The prevailing winds are southwesterly, coming from Africa, and pick up moisture as they cross the Mediterranean. The northern parts of the region have far more rain than the south: about 40 in. (1,000 mm) a year falls in north Lebanon, but only about 5 in. (130 mm) per annum in Gaza. The rain mostly falls on west-facing slopes, while east-facing ones, such as the cliffs above Jericho in the Jordan valley, are in a rain shadow and are consequently arid. Generally, the further east one travels across the region as a whole, the less rain there is.

Rainfall occurs at two seasons. The new year begins in the autumn when the first rains bring fresh life to the parched land after the heat of summer. The gentle 'latter' rains (as they are referred to in the Bible) of late spring arrive in time to help ripen the crops. Winter rains tend to be torrential. For instance, the area around Jerusalem receives about 24 in. (62 cm) of rain per year, roughly the same as, for instance, London. The difference is that whereas in Jerusalem this amount falls on an average of about 50 days and only in winter, in London there can be a steady drizzle all year round.

Such deluges often wash away the surface soil, exposing the bare rock beneath. The problem is worse where the vegetation protecting the soil has been lost through grazing animals (especially goats and sheep) and the felling of trees over the centuries for fuel and building. In the hill country the situation is aggravated by the loss of traditional agricultural terracing. On flat land problems are caused by the use of modern deep-ploughing techniques on soil which is very light and easily blows away if it is not compacted. Today, erosion is a very serious problem for the whole region. Wherever it occurs the water table is lowered and the land rapidly becomes a desert.

The biblical landscape, once fertile and covered with trees, is now, in places, a desolate waste. In Israel, however, a great deal of re-afforestation has been undertaken since the establishment of the new state in 1948. Large areas of pine trees have been created, though in antiquity the hills were blanketed with oak and terebinth. Recently, attempts have been made to recreate the biblical wooded landscape by planting these species, as well as fruit trees, in the Judaean Hills.

The geography of the Levant

The world of the Bible lands centres on the Levant, consisting of Lebanon and Syria in the north, and Israel and Jordan in the south, and, peripherally, the Sinai peninsula. It is a region of extraordinary diversity, both of terrain and climate. Modern Lebanon corresponds to the region called Phoenicia in antiquity, the fertile coastal strip separated from inland Syria by two ranges of mountains and the intervening Bequa'a valley. North of Lebanon the coastal lands of Syria are very productive and support some of the largest Levantine towns of ancient or modern times, such as Antioch, Hama, Aleppo and Homs. Inland Syria is semi-steppe and the only large population centres are at oases such as Damascus or ancient Mari. The southern end of Lebanon is demarcated by a jumble of basalt hills, cutting it off from the hills of upper Galilee. South of Damascus the Golan Heights, the biblical land of Geshur, dominated by the snowy peak of Mt Hermon, overlook the lush plains that lie around the Sea of Galilee.

What's in a name?

The Levant has been known by many names in the course of its history. In the south, the modern state of Israel, occupying much of the land west of the River Jordan, covers most of the territory of the biblical kingdoms of Israel (the northern hill country) and Judah (the southern hills), which was known as Judaea by the Hellenistic era. Most of the hill country is now claimed for a Palestinian Arab state; and Palestine (the word is derived from the Philistines) is perhaps the most enduring name for the whole southern half of the Levant. The coastal strip was not part of the biblical kingdoms but was home to the Canaanites, Philistines and other Sea Peoples.

Several distinct geographical zones run from west to east in the south, the heartland of the Bible. South of Mt Carmel the coastal strip with its sand dunes gives way to the fertile fields of the Sharon valley, with the poorer land of Philistia to the south. East of the latter is the Shephelah, the low southern hills, which produce such good wines. East of the Sharon is the valley of Ayyalon, also very fertile. It rises gently into the Judaean Hills which themselves lead steeply up to Jerusalem. The watershed, at 3,000 ft (915 m), runs along the top of Mt Scopus and the Mt of Olives, just beyond the city. The land then falls away to the east, to the increasingly desert-like conditions of the Judaean Wilderness.

The Jordan valley, which, at around 1,300 ft (395 m) below sea level is the lowest place on the surface of the earth, is an interruption in this terrain. It is bordered on both sides by cliffs which rise steeply to a height of about 3,000 ft (915 m). The valley is part of the great rift system, which runs from eastern Turkey to the East African Rift in Tanzania. Since it is the edge of one of the earth's tectonic plates, it is an area of considerable seismic activity. Transjordan (literally the area beyond the River Jordan) is part of the northern extension of the Arabian steppe. Amman, the capital of the modern kingdom of Jordan, lies on its western edge, on the site of the old Ammonite city, Rabbat Ammon. East of Amman the true desert begins.

Wadis, 'the streams in the dry land' of Psalms 126, 4 are waterless river beds which for most of the year form natural routes for travellers – the 'highways in the desert' of which the prophet spoke (Isaiah 40, 3). Springs just below the surface are marked by lush vegetation, sometimes even a stand of date palms. However, in winter, when rain may be falling many miles distant, torrential floods race down the wadis without warning, sweeping everything away, including the unwary traveller.

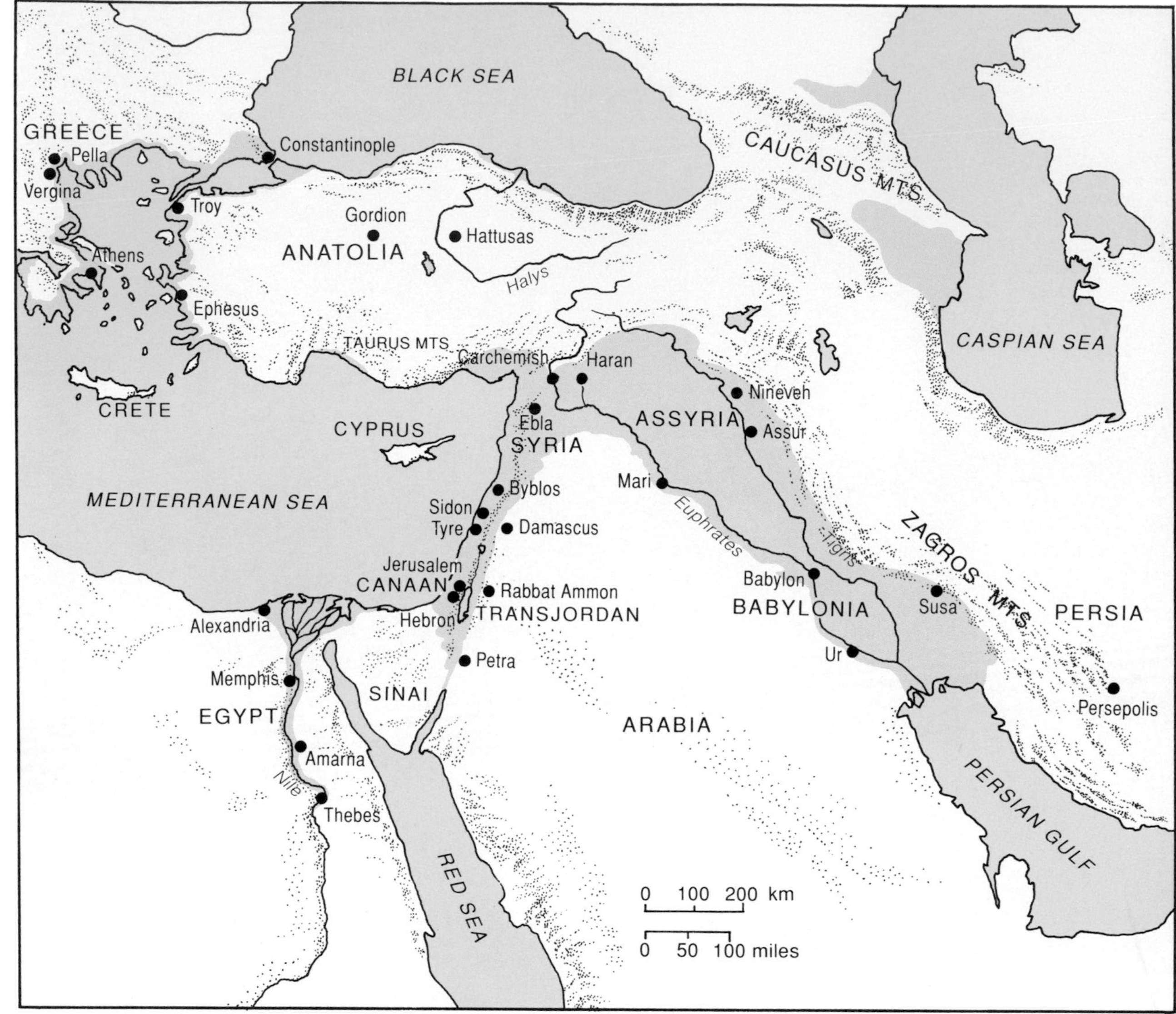

Natural routes of the Near East

The phrase 'the Fertile Crescent' was originally coined to describe the habitable land of the Near East: the area stretching from the Persian Gulf, northwest along the courses of the Tigris and Euphrates, arching west round to the Mediterranean coast and south to Egypt. Although we now know that some people have always lived outside it, the description still fits the area through which most of the great 'trunk roads' passed. In antiquity it was impossible to traverse the waterless deserts of the Arabian steppe. All armies, caravans and nomadic family groups (such as Abraham's) who travelled overland between the Persian Gulf and Egypt had to stay within the boundary of the Fertile Crescent. One of the main caravan cities was Mari, on the Middle Euphrates. From there the caravans made their way to coastal Syria. The oasis of Palmyra became, in late antiquity, an important stopover on this journey. Some routes then led north to Anatolia, others south along the coast. In inland Syria the oasis of Damascus was the most important caravan rendezvous. From here two main routes ran south – the 'Way of the King' (passing east of the Jordan valley into Arabia) and the 'Way of the Sea' (the Roman *Via Maris*). This road crossed the River Jordan north of the Sea of Galilee, past Hazor and across the valley of Esdraelon, and cut through the pass at Megiddo, before following the coast south towards Egypt.

It was the 19th-century scholar Sir Henry Breasted who first coined the expression 'the Fertile Crescent' to describe the swathe of habitable land at the heart of the ancient Near East where some of the earliest civilizations arose. The map (left) shows graphically how this corridor is surrounded by inhospitable areas. All traffic between Egypt in the west and Mesopotamia in the east had to pass through this area. Abraham's family, journeying from Ur in southern Mesopotamia to Mamre (later Hebron) in south Canaan, first had to travel north, to Haran in Syria.

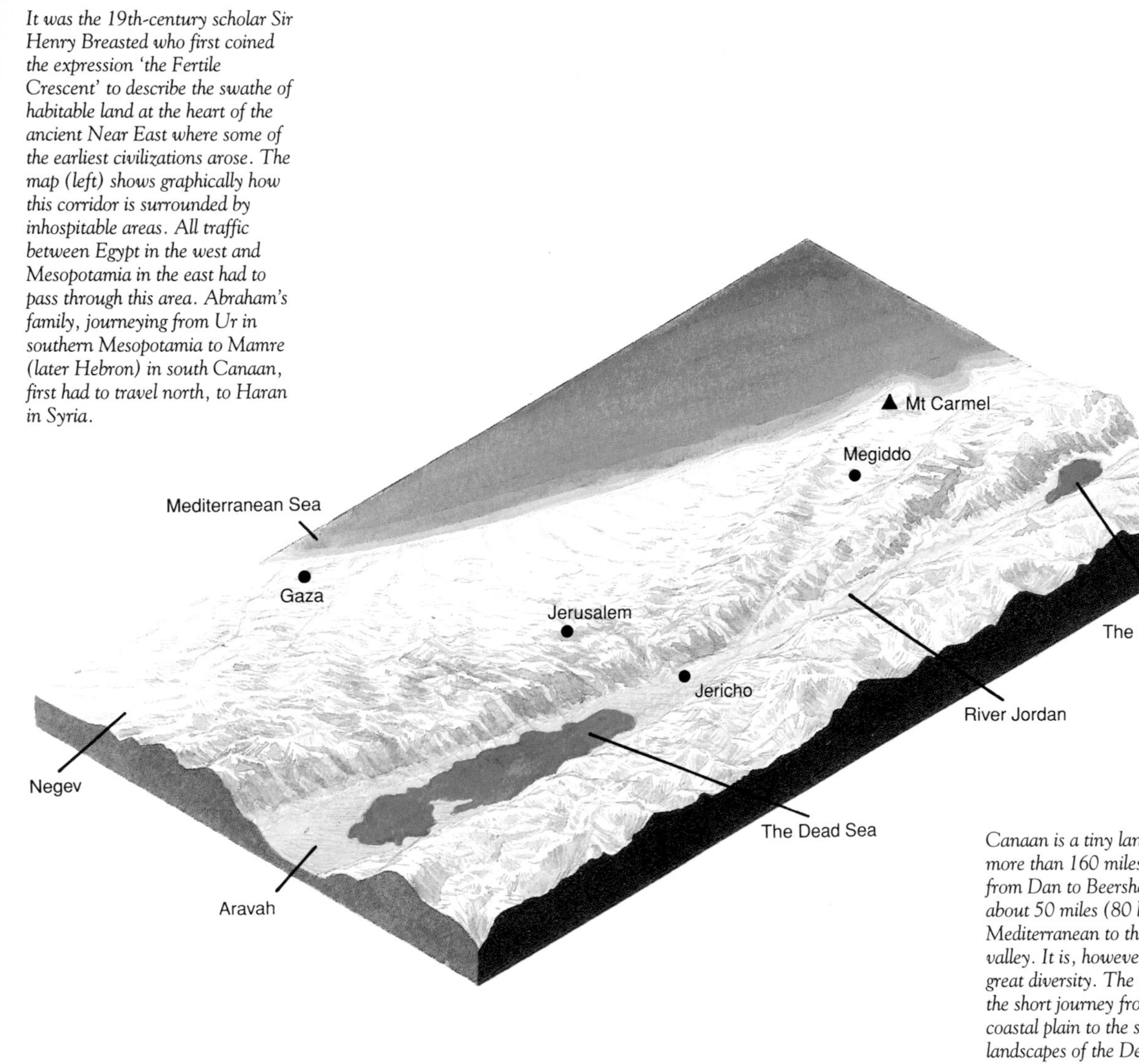

Canaan is a tiny land, not much more than 160 miles (260 km) from Dan to Beersheba and only about 50 miles (80 km) from the Mediterranean to the Jordan valley. It is, however, a land of great diversity. The contrasts on the short journey from the lush coastal plain to the stark landscapes of the Dead Sea, via Jerusalem are very striking.

The strategic nature of the Levant

In essence the Levant is a land bridge between Mesopotamia and Egypt to the north and south, and between Europe and Asia to the west and east, making this area a crossroads of people, trade and ideas. The northern Levant is better favoured in terms of climate and resources – its people learned very early that their cedarwood in particular was much sought after. Most of the trade goods of the Near East were despatched to the Aegean world from the ports of the north of the region. The southern Levant is not as fertile as the north and has few natural resources or good harbours. Its only internationally important trading commodities were olive oil and bitumen. The latter occurs naturally in the Dead Sea area and was used as an adhesive and also in the mummification process in Egypt (*momiya*, hence 'mummy', means bitumen). Foreign influence in the south was much more limited, particularly in the remote and secluded hills, so that their inhabitants were never as wealthy nor as sophisticated.

From ancient times down to the present day the southern Levant has been a buffer zone in international politics. The name of Megiddo, one of its most important cities, has become a byword for the battle which is to take place, according to apocalyptic notions, at the End of Days, between the armies of north and south. Armageddon means 'the hill of Megiddo'.

OUTLINE HISTORY OF THE REGION

FLAVIUS JOSEPHUS

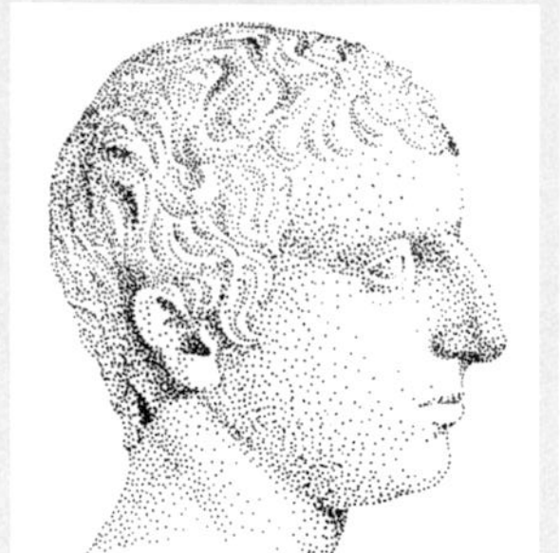

Joseph ben Matthias, later known as Flavius Josephus, was born in AD *37 into a priestly family which traced its origins back to the Hasmonaeans. The bust above, dating to the Roman period, has sometimes been thought to be a portrait of him, though there is no strong evidence for the claim.*

In later life, with the security of Roman citizenship and a rich estate in Judaea, he became comfortably established in Rome in the old home of his patron, the emperor Vespasian. There he devoted himself to scholarship and became the chief apologist of his people, seeking to defend them against the malicious anti-Semitism that was already prevalent.

Everything we know about the life and career of Josephus comes from his own pen. There is little doubt that he was a man of ability, educated in the best Rabbinic academies of his day, as well as a soldier and an historian. His works include The Jewish War *(our main source concerning Herod, as well as the Revolt), and* The Antiquities of the Jews, *which chronicles the history of his people from the Creation to the eve of the revolt in* AD *66. He also wrote* Against Apion, *a defence of the Jews against anti-Semitic propaganda, and an autobiography. Josephus was much respected by the Church Fathers, such as Eusebius and Jerome, who called him 'the Greek Livy'. He wrote in Greek and Aramaic to reach a wide audience and Latin translations were made in the 4th century* AD.

THE WORLD OF THE BIBLE begins with Abraham. He and Sarah stand at the gate of Israel's history as the parents of the nation, entering into the first covenant with the Lord. Although Bible scholars and archaeologists are still engaged in a discussion about the historicity of the man himself (pp. 44–45), the background of the patriarchal world is fixed, in the opinion of many scholars, in the early 2nd millennium BC.

Over 8,000 years separated the era of Abraham and the other patriarchs from the end of the last Ice Age, when the polar ice cap covered most of Europe. During that long period humankind largely ceased to live by hunting and gathering and slowly developed methods of food production. From the 7th millennium BC many groups settled in farming villages wherever climate and soil allowed. Much of the land at that time was covered in forest, the climate was probably milder than today and groundwater resources were more abundant.

Genesis to Exodus

In Mesopotamia and in Egypt urban civilizations evolved in the course of the 4th millennium BC. The reasons behind this are complex, but one stimulus was the development of irrigation agriculture. The social co-operation of large groups of people is necessary for this way of life to succeed; where it does, conditions are in place for advanced cultures to develop. Writing systems were invented in these lands as a means of keeping records in the increasingly complex societies.

The Levant, a fertile corridor between the two opposite poles of Near Eastern civilization, was not as sophisticated as either, although it was open to influence from both. In the north, Syria was much affected by the civilization of Mesopotamia, while the lands to the south were more inclined towards Egypt. Because travel across the waterless desert of the Syrian steppe was impossible in ancient times, all overland journeys between the two great powers had to pass through the Levant corridor and large caravans and powerful armies came and went. In times of stability it was safe for small groups of travellers, such as the patriarchal clans, to make long journeys: the stories of such travels told in Genesis are perfectly feasible.

Egyptian records show that in the first half of the 2nd millennium BC groups of itinerant Semites regularly travelled backwards and forwards across the Sinai desert. Some even managed to gain a strong foothold in the Nile delta in the 18th and 17th centuries BC and became rulers of parts of Egypt at a time of native weakness. A resurgence of Egyptian power came with the princes of Thebes, who became the pharaohs of the 18th Dynasty. The foreign settlers were then no longer welcome and in the middle of the 16th century BC their leaders, known to the Egyptians as the Hyksos, were chased out of the country, mostly back to Canaan. A Semitic peasantry was left behind, some of whom were the ancestors of the Israelites.

About a generation later, the Egyptians under Tuthmosis III (*c.* 1504–1450 BC) consolidated their hold over Canaan. However, during the Amarna period, Egypt's grip on her Levantine empire weakened, but the pharaohs of the 19th Dynasty, starting with Seti I (*c.* 1318–1304 BC), again strengthened their grasp on Canaan. Along the desert roads of Sinai, called the Ways of Horus, they established a series of key fortresses, including Gaza in the south of Canaan. Further north they established an important garrison at Beth Shean in the Esdraelon valley, not far from Megiddo.

Ramesses II (*c.* 1304–1237 BC) is generally considered to be the pharaoh of the Exodus, when the Israelites made their escape from Egypt under the leadership of Moses. Making their way to Canaan took them the whole of the Exodus generation. The first reference to a people called 'Israel' settled in the land of Canaan is found on the Stela of the Year 5 of Merneptah (*c.* 1236–1223 BC), the successor of Ramesses II. Thus Israel was recognized by this time as a distinct entity, settled in Canaan.

Other newcomers to the land of Canaan

The 13th century saw increasing numbers of would-be settlers, quite alien to the Near East, making their way southwards through the Levant by land and sea. These people are known to us as the 'Sea Peoples', because that is one of their names in Egyptian texts. Before the 13th century BC groups arriving in smaller numbers had been absorbed into Egyptian society, often employed as mercenary soldiers.

Soon, however, the sheer weight of their numbers became too great. Cities, kingdoms, empires collapsed before them and during the 13th century BC the entire fabric of Late Bronze Age civilization in the Levant, Asia Minor, Syria and Egypt was torn apart.

One group of Sea Peoples settled along the coast of the extreme south of the Levant and became familiar to the writers of the Bible as the Philistines. Their characteristic pottery is found widely distributed in southern Canaan in the 11th century BC as they began to expand from the coastal region inland and northwards through the hills of southern Canaan. Here they came into conflict with the Israelites in the first phase of their settlement. Saul could not contain them; but David could, and did, apparently with ease.

David (*c.* 1004–965 BC), the shepherd boy who became the father of a long line of kings of Judah, also achieved the unification of the 12 tribes of Israel. By taking Jerusalem from the Jebusites and making it his capital he began the long association between his people and the city, establishing a united kingdom of Israel and Judah.

David's united kingdom did not long outlast the reign of his son, Solomon (*c.* 965–928 BC) who built the Temple in Jerusalem. After Solomon, the kingdom split into two: Israel in the north and Judah in the south. The next centuries were filled with war as the great empires of Assyria and Babylonia strove with Egypt for supremacy. The biblical kingdoms situated between them were often caught up in these struggles and suffered thereby. First Israel succumbed to the Assyrians in 721 BC, and then Judah fell to Nebuchadnezzar of Babylon in 587 BC. The Judaeans, like the people of Israel before them, were sent into exile.

The Judaean exiles in Babylon, however, not only survived the experience but even gained by it. It was in the exilic community that they developed fresh religious philosophies to meet the new challenges to their continued existence as followers of the Lord. Concepts of monotheism and personal responsibility were forged; ideas at the heart of Judaism and, later, Christianity and Islam. When Cyrus, king of the Persians, who succeeded the Babylonians as overlords of the region, allowed the exiles, who now could truly be called Jews, to return home in 538 BC, it was with renewed faith that they built the Second Temple in Jerusalem.

The arrival of Hellenism in the Near East had a great impact on the peoples of the area and was the next threat to the Jews. Alexander's armies brought the Greek language and the Greek way of life to the Near East in the late 4th century BC, and nothing was to be the same again. Among the Jews some were enthusiastic supporters of the new culture, others were vehemently opposed to it. So great was the split within the community in Judaea that when the edict of the Syrian king, Antiochus IV (175–164 BC), forbade the practice of Judaism on pain of torture and death, not all the people rose against him. But many did and eventually, after a long and bloody revolution, an independent Jewish kingdom was established under the Hasmonaean kings.

Within a very short time corruption, political assassinations and disputes over succession in the Hasmonaean kingdom led to the arrival on the scene of Rome, in the shape of Pompey. It was vital that the Romans held the lands of the eastern Mediterranean seaboard against their enemy, Parthia, to the east. Needing a loyal and stable leadership in Judaea they appointed to the throne the most able man they could find. This was not a member of the Hasmonaean family, but Herod, an Idumaean, whose family had been forcibly converted to Judaism less than a century earlier. Herod the Great (37–4 BC) proved a wise choice in many ways. He was a capable ruler, loyal ally and gifted businessman. He was also a murderer of several of his own family as well as many of his subjects and became increasingly feared by his people as his reign progressed. When he died the nation rejoiced, but he left for posterity some of the most extravagant and outstanding buildings of the Roman east.

Jesus and Christianity

Jesus was probably born in the year that Herod the Great died, and his life changed human perception of God and the course of history in the western world. The classic form of Christianity, however, was created after his death, by another Jew, Paul of Tarsus, who began the work of preaching the news of Christ to Gentiles as well as to Jews.

Jewish resentment of their Roman masters exploded in the First and Second Jewish Revolts (AD 66–73 and 132–35). Following the Second Revolt Jews were forbidden entry to Jerusalem. The Emperor Hadrian rebuilt the city as a Roman colony, naming it Aelia Capitolina after his family clan, Aelius. The emperor also gave orders for pagan temples to be built in places hallowed by Christians for their association with Jesus. The centre of the Apostolic church moved to Rome, but in the

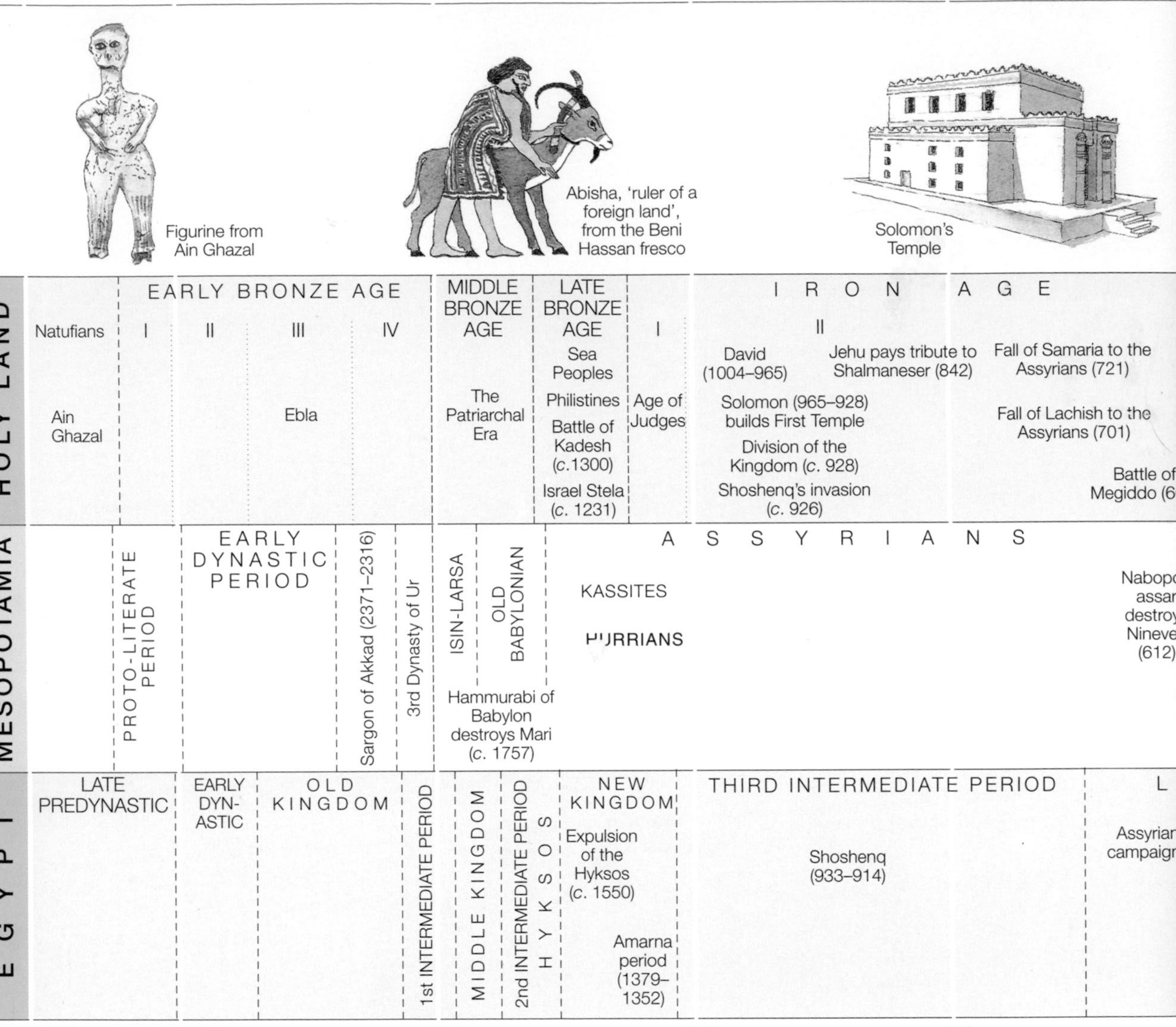

A simplified timeline of the main cultures, peoples and events connected with the Bible lands.

land of Jesus' birth Christianity was all but eradicated for about three centuries.

Byzantine Christianity

Christianity returned to the Holy Land in the mid-4th century AD with Queen Helena, the mother of the emperor Constantine (AD 306–37). She was entrusted with identifying the holy places connected with Jesus. Thereafter Christianity flourished in Palestine until the Islamic conquest of the early 7th century AD. The capital city of the Islamic Ummayad dynasty was Damascus. At first, considerable tolerance was shown by the new rulers of the Levant to both their Jewish and Christian subjects. The Dome of the Rock was built in the late 7th century AD, on the Temple platform, which had probably stood empty since the Roman destruction of Herod's Temple in AD 70.

By the end of the 10th century AD the Fatimids, the Shi'ite rulers of Egypt, had gained control of the Holy Land. Al-Hakim (AD 996–1021) instituted a reign of terror, during which he ordered the destruction of the Church of the Holy Sepulchre in Jerusalem, which ultimately set in train the events which led to the Crusades.

At the approach of the millennium excitement mounted in Europe, as Christians foresaw the end of the present age and the second coming of the Messiah. Pilgrims travelled in ever

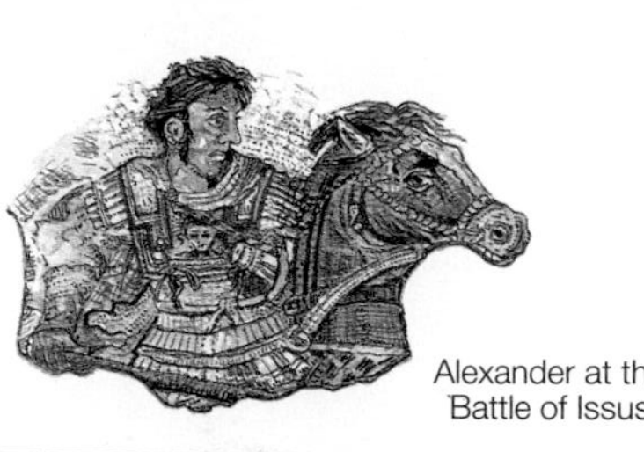

Alexander at the Battle of Issus

Detail of the Arch of Titus

PERSIAN	[...] of Jerusalem to [...]ebuchadnezzar (587); Return of the exiles from Babylon (538); Dedication of Second Temple (515)
HELLENISTIC	Alexander defeats Darius at Issus (333); Battle of Ipsus (301), Ptolemaic rule; Battle of Panias (200), Seleucid rule; Maccabean Revolt (167); Hasmonaean Kingdom (142); Pompey enters Jerusalem (63); Herod becomes king (40)
ROMAN	Death of Herod (4); Birth of Jesus (*c.* 4); First Jewish Revolt (66–70); Titus captures Jerusalem (70); Fall of Masada (73); Second Jewish Revolt (132–135)
BYZANTINE	Persians capture Jerusalem (614); Arab conquest of Jerusalem (638)
ISLAMIC	Crusaders capture Jerusalem (1099); Crusaders expelled by the Mamelukes (1291); Ottoman rule (1516); Allenby enters Jerusalem (1917); State of Israel (1948)

PERSIAN	Fall of Babylon to Cyrus (539)
HELLENISTIC	Alexander dies at Babylon (323)
PARTHIANS	
SASSANIANS	
ISLAMIC	Haroun al-Raschid caliph of Baghdad (786)

PERIOD	Persian rule (525–404); Persian rule (343–332)
PTOLEMAIC PERIOD	Alexander crowned pharaoh (332); Septuagint written in Alexandria; Battle of Actium (31)
ROMAN RULE	
BYZANTINE	
ISLAMIC	Saladin becomes ruler (1171)

400 — 200 — BC/AD — 1000 — 2000

greater numbers to the Holy Land. The First Crusade began officially on 27 November 1095. In a rabble-rousing speech Pope Urban II, outside the walls of Clermont in France, urged the peoples of Christendom to rescue the holy city of Jerusalem from the Moslem hordes. The Crusaders had a much worse effect on the region than the Moslems whom they supplanted. Because of the Crusaders' inability to recognize their co-religionists, the local Christian communities were in more danger from them than their Moslem overlords. In spite of the magnificent castles which are their lasting glory, by the time the Crusaders set sail from the Holy Land for the last time in 1291 the region was well rid of them.

The Mamelukes, who began as slave recruits in the cavalry of the Egyptian sultan and eventually took over the kingdom, gained control of Palestine in around 1255. Under their rule it became something of a backwater for several centuries, but with the coming of the Ottoman Turks in 1516 the situation improved. The city walls built by the Ottoman sultan Suleiman the Magnificent around Jerusalem are still standing and are very familiar in paintings and photographs today.

The Ottomans remained the rulers of Palestine until the beginning of the 20th century, when Britain was officially entrusted by the League of Nations with the Mandate there following the First World War.

WOMEN TRAVELLERS

Lady Hester Stanhope in local costume.

CAROLINE OF BRUNSWICK
After Helena in the 4th century AD, *the next royal lady to travel in the Holy Land arrived soon after the turn of the 19th century. Caroline of Brunswick (1768–1821) had married her first cousin, the Prince of Wales ('Prinny') in 1795. Unfortunately the royal couple took an immediate dislike to each other and they separated formally in 1796, soon after the birth of their daughter, Princess Charlotte. In 1814 Princess Caroline decided to go abroad. With a small retinue she made her way across Europe to Greece and eventually reached the Holy Land. There she visited almost all the holy places. Her itinerary included the Galilee, where she stayed for a short time in Nazareth, the Jordan valley, stopping at Jericho and the Dead Sea, and, finally, Jerusalem. By the time one of her companions published an account of her travels in 1821, the self-styled Queen of England was dead. She died a few days after having been dramatically turned away from the doors of Westminster Abbey during her husband's coronation.*

Wady Mousa – at length we have arrived and it is worth all the long way. We descended to the village of Wady Mousa...rode on and soon got into the entrance of the defile that leads to Petra....We went on in ecstasies until suddenly between the narrow opening of the rocks, we saw the most beautiful sight I have ever seen.

Gertrude Bell, Diaries, 29 March 1900

THE HOLY LAND AND THE COUNTRIES around it have attracted visitors from numerous places throughout the ages. Many of them on their return home have published accounts of their travels, complete with maps, illustrations and, from the 19th century on, photographs. Among these visitors there has been a surprising number of women, some of them travelling alone – surprising because the region has been considered generally unsafe for any foreigners, let alone women, for many centuries.

Queen Helena

The first recorded woman traveller was Helena, in the 4th century AD. She was the mother of the Roman emperor, Constantine, who commissioned her to travel to Palestine and identify the holy places associated with the life of Christ. The sites she sought were often revealed to her in dreams, and she founded churches, shrines and monasteries at these spots. Several of her identifications are likely to be historically accurate, including the Church of the Holy Sepulchre in Jerusalem and the Basilica of the Nativity in Bethlehem. If, as some scholars believe, there is a grain of truth in the stories of the Empress finding the True Cross in Jerusalem, together with the nails used in the Crucifixion, then Helena can even be said to be the first archaeologist in the Holy Land.

Egeria

A few decades later, but still in the 4th century AD, a nun whose name is thought to have been Egeria left her quiet convent life somewhere in the western Mediterranean and made her way to the Holy Land. She spent several years on her travels, joining groups of other pilgrims to reach many of the holy places. She stayed for some time in Constantinople and for at least three years, perhaps AD 381–84, in Jerusalem. While based there she made many trips to places of Christian interest, including the Galilee, where she visited Nazareth, Transjordan, where she made the ascent of Mt Nebo, and Antioch and Edessa in Syria. She also travelled to Egypt, probably twice, and made the difficult journey into Sinai, in order to stand on the mountain where it was believed that Moses received the Ten Commandments. By her day this had already been identified as Santa Katerina in the south of the peninsula.

Egeria wrote down all her experiences for the sisters of her convent at home. Miraculously, a part of her work has survived, in manuscript form, bound in with another work and discovered in a monastery library in Arezzo, Italy, in 1884. It is a great pity that no more than half of her account has survived because it is the best source of information not only for the eastern church of her day, but also for the topography of the Holy Land and other countries she travelled through at this early period. She wrote in haphazard Latin mixed with Greek expressions picked up on her travels. An energetic individual and an indefatigable traveller, Egeria was a pilgrim of strong constitution and an endlessly enquiring mind.

Lady Hester Stanhope

For the next 1,300 years there were apparently no women travellers of note who reached Palestine, until Lady Hester Stanhope (1776–1839). She was a genuine British eccentric: deeply romantic, but at the same time with a pragmatic approach to life which left her with no patience with the female social inhibitions of her class and day. The niece of the English Prime Minister William Pitt, she acted as his housekeeper and hostess until his death in 1806. Although she was then given a royal pension by King George III, she was unable to settle back into the life of a private lady and left England for the Levant in 1810. Once there, she took up residence in a dilapidated castle in a remote village in the Lebanese mountains until her death.

During her time in the Levant she adopted the male costume of the region which, so she said, was preferable to wearing the veil of a woman. She dabbled in the politics of the area and bullied everyone in her vicinity, while keeping open house for all European visitors. From her base she travelled widely and there is, for instance, a picturesque account of her entry into Palmyra. In 1815 she obtained a permit to dig for buried treasure at Ashkelon. Her workmen found a colossal ancient statue, but she had it destroyed, saying that she did not wish to be accused of hunting for curios to 'steal' for the British, as had happened only recently to Lord Elgin in connection with the marbles from the Parthenon in Athens.

Mary Eliza Rogers

In the 19th century many Europeans went to Palestine, then under Ottoman rule. Among them were missionaries, doctors, diplomats, geographers and explorers. Almost all of them had an interest in the biblical heritage of the land and its inhabitants. Many women came with their husbands, brothers or fathers, and one in particular has left an interesting memoir of her stay. Mary Eliza Rogers accompanied her diplomat brother to Palestine in the 1850s. She had access to the harems of the houses her brother visited and wrote detailed studies of the women she encountered. Her insights into the confined lives of the women, who were ignorant of virtually everything beyond the harem walls, make fascinating reading. She travelled widely throughout Palestine with her brother and met not only Arab women, but also those of the Samaritan, Druze and Jewish communities. Often considered by the men she met as an 'honorary man', she was also in some respects a typical Victorian lady, always obedient to the wishes of her brother, whom she obviously adored.

Women travellers in the 20th century

In the 20th century there have been several distinguished women visitors to the Holy Land. Gertrude Bell (1868–1926) fell in love with the Near East during the winter of 1899, which she spent in Jerusalem learning Arabic. Before the First World War she spent many years travelling in the deserts of the Near East, getting to know the people who lived there, and wrote several books about her experiences. She was also a considerable photographer and her pictures of archaeological sites – some of which she excavated – are particularly valuable today as records both of places that have changed considerably and a way of life that has disappeared. In 1923 she was appointed to the British High Commission in Baghdad as Oriental Secretary and was the first Director of Antiquities in Iraq. On her death she left money to found the British School of Archaeology in Iraq.

Rose Macaulay, like Gertrude Bell, was a graduate of Oxford University, where she took a degree in history. She travelled widely in the Levant and some of her novels, such as *The Towers of Trebizond*, have a Near Eastern background. Her most famous travel book, *The Pleasure of Ruins*, was published in 1953 and contains a great deal of perceptive writing on places she visited in the Levant.

No account of women travellers in the Near East would be complete without mentioning Dame Freya Stark, who died in 1993 at the age of 100. One of her many books about her travels, *Alexander's Path*, is a classic of adventure. It recounts her journey through Turkey as, travelling completely alone and for the most part relying on erratic buses, she followed the trail of Alexander the Great across the country. She also learned Arabic and in 1927 journeyed from Venice to Beirut, where she spent a year touring Lebanon and Syria. In 1929 she visited Baghdad and returned to the Near East on numerous occasions after that.

Gertrude Bell outside her tent in Babylon, in 1909. This is a rare photograph of her as she generally preferred to be behind the camera rather than in front of it.

ARCHAEOLOGISTS IN THE HOLY LAND

Lieutenant Charles Warren (right) being presented with a Samaritan book by Yakub es-Shellaby, the Samaritan leader, at the foot of Mt Gerizim. After his work in Palestine, Warren returned to England and became Police Commissioner in London, where he was in charge of the hunt for Jack the Ripper, the murderer who terrorized the city in 1888.

Not for the greed of gold
Not for the hope of fame
Not for a lasting heritage
Not for a far-flung name.
Rather for making history
And for some lore of old
That is our aim and object
Not for the greed of gold!

THIS CAMP SONG of the young and idealistic archaeologists who were 'Petrie's Pups' at Tell Farah on the edge of the Negev desert in Palestine in the 1920s, well illustrates the pioneering spirit of the period. By that time there had been great interest in the Holy Land in Britain and the USA for the best part of a century, inspired in both countries by a strong Christian conviction.

From the early part of the 19th century serious explorers began to arrive in Palestine. One of the most eminent among them was the American historical geographer, Edward Robinson (1794–1863), who succeeded in accurately identifying many biblical sites as he travelled around the country, in 1838 and again in 1852. In the 1850s Dean Arthur Stanley (1815–81) published his best-selling reminiscences of his travels in Palestine. Such scholarly work laid the basis for the later surveying, mapping and excavation of Palestine.

In 1865 an Englishman, Captain Charles Wilson (1836–1905) of the Royal Engineers, led an Ordnance Survey expedition to Jerusalem in order to make an accurate survey of the city. The success of this venture raised public interest in the Holy Land to new heights in England, and in the same year the Palestine Exploration Fund (p. 20) was established under the patronage of Queen Victoria. Scientific investigations on behalf of the Fund began with the work of Lieutenant Charles Warren (1840–1927) in Jerusalem in 1867, and continued most notably with the Survey of Western Palestine between 1871 and 1877. From July 1872 this work was led by Lieutenant Claude Conder (1848–1910), and its most famous participant was Lieutenant H.H. Kitchener (later Lord Kitchener of Khartoum; 1850–1916). The Survey was the most important contribution made by the British to the archaeology of Palestine in the 19th century. The results were published as a series of 26 sheets of 1-in. maps, covering 6,000 sq. miles. These maps have, until very recently, been the yardstick by which all other maps of the region have been measured and their value for archaeologists and geographers has not diminished over time.

The American Palestine Exploration Society was formed in 1870 and paralleled the work of the British society by conducting a Survey of Eastern Palestine. Unfortunately, the task proved impossible in the face of much local opposition east of the Jordan and the Society was disbanded soon after.

Sir William Flinders Petrie (1852–1943) was the true pioneer of excavation in Palestine with his expedition to Tell el-Hesi in 1890. He was the first to realize that pottery types could be dated according to the layers in a tell. Petrie's greatest love was Egypt, but he returned to Palestine more than 30 years later, by which time he was over 70 years old. Even so, over the next 10 years he conducted several major excavations as well as some smaller ones.

Early 20th-century excavators

In 1920 the British set up the first Department of Antiquities in Palestine, directed by John Garstang (1876–1956), who was then head of the newly founded British School of

Archaeology in Jerusalem. The Palestine Archaeological Museum (now called the Rockefeller) opened in 1939, by which time there were many competent excavators working in Palestine. This was the era of the large, well-funded expeditions set up to excavate the major tells. It was also the period when biblical archaeology was fashionable. Archaeologists and Bible scholars regularly interpreted their findings in the light of biblical history.

This approach did not recommended itself to Kathleen Kenyon (1906–78), the leading British archaeologist of the day (p. 38). She had been trained in field techniques in Britain by the formidable Mortimer Wheeler and she brought his methods to bear on the problems of Palestinian archaeology. She excavated first at Samaria, where she took part in the joint Anglo-American excavations of the 1930s. Her greatest work was undoubtedly at Jericho from 1951 to 1958. The Jericho dig was seminal in the development of excavation techniques in Israel. She also excavated in Jerusalem between 1961 and 1967, principally south of the Temple Mount in the area now known as the City of David.

Britain was not the only country interested in the archaeology of the Holy Land. Individuals and expeditions from all over the world undertook excavations at many sites for over a century. Foremost among these were the Americans, such as the Oriental Institute of Chicago, with an expedition to Megiddo, or W.F. Albright (p. 20) who worked at Tell Beit Mirsim. After the Second World War the pace of exploration increased. American and British archaeologists have retained their high profile, but numerous other nationalities are represented – including Canadian, Dutch, French, German, Japanese and many more.

Israeli archaeologists

Since 1945 a generation of Israeli excavators has grown up with an especially passionate interest in the biblical period and a deep knowledge of the Bible in its original landscape and language. Many chose to specialize in the Iron Age, which was the setting for much of the Old Testament and largely corresponds to the First Temple Period. Yigael Yadin (1917–84) was one of the great figures of Israeli archaeology. Along with others, he was inclined to interpret his findings in line with biblical events, confident that archaeology could throw light on biblical history. Another notable figure is Yohanan Aharoni (1919–76), a historical-geographer and one of the principal archaeologists less bound by the biblical text and thus more objective in their use of archaeological data.

An important development for Israeli archaeology was the reformation of the Israel Department of Antiquities into the independent Israel Antiquities Authority. Many sites are currently being restored so that they can be enjoyed and understood by a wider public and salvage work is undertaken where construction is scheduled. Although there is concern that restoration work may go too far, and that unsuitable methods may be used, there is no doubt that there will be a great benefit in bringing the past within reach of more people.

SIR WILLIAM FLINDERS PETRIE

William Petrie (seen here at Tell Farah South), the British archaeologist, was primarily interested in Egypt. However, the Palestine Exploration Fund, having decided on a programme of field archaeology outside Jerusalem, appointed him to excavate on their behalf in 1890. Petrie chose the site of Tell el-Hesi, in southern Palestine, and spent a six-week season there in 1890. His choice was partly influenced by the fact that a natural section had been cut through the layers of debris on the west side of the tell by the floodwaters of a wadi. Petrie could therefore take samples of pottery and objects from each layer with little effort or disturbance. From these he constructed a relative sequence of pottery for the site, and then extended it to the whole of Palestine. He also compared Egyptian objects from the tell with similar ones he had found in Egypt and whose dates were known. In this way he was able to date the Hesi levels – the method is known as cross-dating – and established a chronology for ancient Palestine. Although his conclusions have since been modified, the method itself is still in universal use.

Petrie spent only one season in Palestine before returning to Egypt. But he did train a whole generation of young archaeologists who subsequently worked in Palestine. Among these was the American, Frederick Bliss, who excavated at Tell el-Hesi from 1891 to 1893 and in Jerusalem between 1894 and 1897.

THE BIBLE AND ARCHAEOLOGY

WILLIAM FOXWELL ALBRIGHT

Albright (1891–1971) was an extraordinary polymath: an archaeologist, Bible scholar, linguist and historian. The essence of his work was to set the Bible and its history into its context as a part of the cultural environment of the ancient Near East. This was the theme of his most important book, From Stone Age to Christianity, *which traced the development of monotheism. As a young man he considered the Bible primarily as a piece of literature, without a basis in historical fact; but his views gradually changed and he became the greatest proponent of its historicity.*

His most important experience as a field archaeologist was at Tell Beit Mirsim in southern Palestine, where he dug in the 1930s. He applied the archaeological chronology which he established at that site to the whole country, using the framework of Stone, Bronze and Iron Ages. In his book The Archaeology of Palestine *he put forward his conviction that archaeology and the Bible are essentially consistent with each other. His was the most important influence on a whole generation of scholars. Dissenting voices were rarely heard during his lifetime and contrary opinions gained little credence until after his death.*

THE NOTION OF BIBLICAL ARCHAEOLOGY is to some extent an outmoded one. It relied on the 19th-century assumption, perpetuated in the middle of the 20th century by W.F. Albright, that archaeological excavations could prove the literal truth of the Bible narrative. No expert in the field of either Bible study or the archaeology of the Near East, especially in the Levant, would deny that archaeology can illuminate the biblical narrative (for instance, the siege of Lachish – pp. 92–95) and even confirm details of the biblical text. Concern arises only if insistence on the absolute historical accuracy of the Bible is such that, even unwittingly, it obscures the objective interpretation of the archaeological evidence.

It is very interesting to compare the 'statements of intent' of the similarly named Palestine Exploration Fund in London and the Palestine Exploration Society in New York, set up within five years of each other (1865 and 1870 respectively). The tasks which they set themselves were comparable, but their ideologies were clearly worlds apart. The objectives of the former were: 'the accurate and systematic investigation of the archaeology, topography, geology and physical geography, natural history, manners and customs of the Holy Land, for biblical illustration.'

Frontispiece of the Palestine Exploration Quarterly, *showing Warren's shaft and tunnels dug below the Temple Mount in 1870.*

In America the committee of the PES had quite different aims: 'the illustration and defense of the Bible – whatever goes to verify the Bible as real...is a refutation of unbelief. The Committee feels that they have in trust a sacred service for science and for religion.'

Thus, at the outset of archaeological investigations in Palestine, two quite different ideals, which may be defined as the secular and the sacred, were at work.

Albright and after

It has often been said that adherents of biblical archaeology travelled the Holy Land with a Bible in one hand and a spade in the other. Perhaps this is a little exaggerated, but there is a grain of truth in it. Rabbi Nelson Glueck, (1901–71), famous for his pioneering surveys in Jordan and in the Negev, always interpreted archaeological results with respect to the Bible. G.E. Wright (1909–74), the excavator of Shechem and the founding editor of the influential journal *Biblical Archaeologist*, was another enthusiastic supporter of the idea that the Bible and archaeology were always at one.

It was only after the death of Albright in 1971 that dissenting voices gathered strength and facts that did not fit the theories of biblical archaeology began to be re-examined. One of the central problems was that of Jericho and its supposed destruction by the Israelites under Joshua. In accordance with the Bible, Albright advocated a view of the Israelite arrival as a conquest, which took place, he believed, in the 13th century BC. Kenyon's work at Jericho, however, found little trace of a settlement at this period, and none of a destruction. The Bible, it is now realized, cannot be taken as objective history, and most archaeologists today agree with the position of H.J. Franken that their labours are quite separate from those of Bible scholars.

Ironically, it was Franken's own excavations at Tell Deir 'Alla in the Jordan valley that brought to light an inscription mentioning Balaam. The Bible relates how Balaam, at the bidding of Balak, king of Moab, tried to curse the Israelites as they reached the Promised Land but was only able to bless them, at the

Lord's command (Numbers 23–24). Thus the very archaeologist who has had severe doubts about the relevance of archaeology to the Bible is the one who has found this very important reference to an early figure in the Old Testament.

This, perhaps, is the moral of the story, since clearly archaeology can be relevant to the biblical text. The point is that archaeology and Bible study are two separate disciplines which sometimes have a direct bearing on each other. As an archaeological tool the Bible should be treated as rigorously as any other documentary source. Archaeological findings may help the Bible scholar, but ultimately the scriptures are concerned with theology and theological, rather than objective, history.

Current preoccupations and the way ahead

As archaeologists today realize, the biblical period was just one era in the several thousand years of human history and prehistory in the Levant. Many other topics and times are now under investigation. Progress is being made, particularly in regions and periods previously little studied, such as the kingdom of Jordan, or the later Islamic era. Archaeologists are now looking forward to a time when it will be possible for scholars on both sides of the present political divide to become full colleagues in the work of reconstructing the archaeology and ancient history of the whole region – a task which makes the arguments for and against biblical archaeology seem small by comparison.

In recent years there has also been a move away from the preoccupation with the First Temple Period. Both Israeli archaeologists and their foreign colleagues now have a higher degree of interest in questions which do not relate only to the Bible. A completely new approach to the sets of questions which can be addressed by archaeology has emerged. Emphasis now is often placed on the reconstruction of ancient ways of life, frequently by reference to traditional customs of Palestine during the Ottoman period. Other interests include settlement patterns and ancient demography.

James L. Starkey, the excavator of Lachish, pointing to the exact findspot of the famous Lachish Letters, in the debris of the gatehouse of Level II, destroyed in 587 BC *by Nebuchadnezzar.*

Archaeology can provide background information about situations known from the Bible. The nature of this information, however, is inherently different from the biblical information – it does not have a message. The Bible presents historical events in the light of a very specific religious interpretation, which archaeological situations do not possess.

H.J. Franken, *Palestine Excavation Quarterly* 1976, pp. 10–11

Biblical theology and Biblical archaeology must go hand in hand if we are to comprehend the Bible's meaning.

G.E. Wright, *Biblical Archaeologist* 1957, p. 17

The Tale of a Tell

And Pharaoh commanded the same day the taskmasters of the people and their officers saying, Ye shall no more give the people straw to make bricks as heretofore: let them go and gather straw for themselves.
Exodus 5, 6–7

MANY OF THE MAJOR archaeological sites in the Near East are visible as mounds standing well above the level of the surrounding countryside. Such a site is called a *tell* in Arabic-speaking countries, *tepe* in Iran or *hüyük* in Turkey. Whereas in Europe and America archaeologists are accustomed to start work from the present-day surface and dig down to the past, in the Near East they usually have to climb high above ground level to begin excavating. Tells represent the accumulation of centuries of occupation debris formed mainly from the decay of structures made of mud brick, with some use of stone, usually as foundations. Mud bricks, made of earth mixed with water and straw and left in the sun to dry, were the basic building blocks in the ancient Near East, and are still used in some places. While simple and easy to make, mud brick decomposes very quickly and the average life of a mud-brick building is only about 30 years, although with good upkeep it may last longer. If a building or settlement was destroyed by fire, the conflagration baked the mud bricks, making the resulting layers of debris almost indestructible.

The characteristic shape of a tell is round or oval, with sloping sides. With each successive period of building the mound grows higher, the sides steeper and the habitable area on top smaller. Foundations for new city walls were almost always dug inside the line of previous defences for stability. To prevent erosion and to deny attackers an easy foothold, the sloping sides of tells were often encased in a thick layer of plaster, bonded into the slope for strength and sometimes laid over a secure foundation of

Tell Beersheba from the air, showing the areas of excavation. The steep sides of the tell were formed by the creation of a plaster glacis, laid over boulders. At least two city walls were exposed in the deep section trench visible on the left, where the excavators 'sliced' through the defences in order to uncover their sequence.

small boulders. This type of defensive system is called a *glacis* and is the main reason for the distinctive shape of tells. At the top stood a defensive wall, strongly built of mud brick on stone footings. The glacis was usually revetted by another wall at its foot. The origin of this system can be traced to Early Bronze Age cities, as confirmed by recent finds at Tell Jarmuth, southwest of Jerusalem.

A second type of fortification was the rampart. Mounds of earth were thrown up against both sides of a rubble core, effectively sandwiching it between them. Sometimes the ramparts were crowned by a defensive wall. Huge expanses were enclosed in this way: the area within the ramparts of the lower city of Hazor is about 200 acres (80 ha) and in Syria some are even larger: those at Qatna enclose about 250 acres (100 ha). Their construction was probably a communal effort – reminiscent of the rebuilding of the walls of Jerusalem after the Babylonian Exile (p. 108).

Building techniques

The rarity of stone and timber made them valuable commodities in the ancient Near East. Stone was, for the most part, limited to foundations and the ornamentation of palaces, as in Mesopotamia, or temples, as in Egypt. In the Levant ashlar masonry, that is, finely-cut, rectangular monumental stone blocks, was mainly reserved for prestigious royal or public buildings. The lower courses of the walls of such buildings might be faced with plain or decorated stone panels called orthostats. By Hellenistic and Roman times, when rulers had huge numbers of slaves at their disposal, massive structures such as fortresses or theatres might be built entirely of stone. Timber long and strong enough to be used for roofing material or general building purposes was expensive. This stimulated the development of the arch and the dome (originally in mud brick, later in stone), which are now such characteristic features of Islamic architecture.

Identifying archaeological sites

One of the most frequent queries put to archaeologists is 'How do you know where to dig?'. The answer has changed over the past decades as the theoretical questions asked by archaeologists themselves and the field techniques at their disposal have become increasingly sophisticated. Up to the Second World War, the great tell sites of the Near East, such as Kuyunjik (ancient Nineveh) in Mesopotamia, or Beth Shean and Megiddo, in Palestine, were obvious choices for archaeological expeditions for wealthy institutions in the west. At Megiddo the stated aim of the American archaeological team working there in the 1930s was to strip the tell, layer by layer, down to bedrock. The Americans did indeed remove a large part of the tell, discovering much useful information about the early periods which would not otherwise be available. However, a great deal of the site remains for future investigation. Today, excavation is not the only way of investigating sites and archaeologists are aware of the fact that excavating a site also destroys it. Wherever possible, archaeologists dig only when necessary, due to threats to a site or to solve specific problems, and leave much of it untouched for future researchers.

Large-scale excavations are usually expensive and since the 1970s archaeologists have turned their attention to smaller projects, such as sites occupied only for a short period. In such places one or two seasons of work can often throw light on an aspect of particular interest to the excavators.

Regional surveys, aiming to locate all the ancient sites within a specific area, such as a valley, plain or range of hills, are now carried out alongside the more traditional site surveys, which simply examine a single site for datable material. An individual site is considered as a part of its surroundings – not just its general environment, the basis of its economy and so forth, but also its relationship to other sites – for instance, whether it was a farm complex dependent on a nearby hamlet, a specialist settlement such as a potters' village or a city ruling outlying towns.

Landscape archaeology

Since the 1980s landscape archaeology has become very popular. One scholar has described this approach as 'total archaeology' – the examination of a given area in every respect and throughout time, from the earliest days up to and including the present. Although very comprehensive, it is not particularly expensive to undertake and can be carried out with a very small team of investigators. Everything in an area is carefully studied, mapped and dated: field systems; agricultural terracing; isolated installations such as wine or oil presses; animal pens; walls and all other artificial structures. Studies are made of soil types; land-use and industry; cemeteries and burial practices; water sources and transport routes to gain a complete picture of the region. Actual digging is just one of the tools available

Deir el-Balah, excavated by the Israeli archaeologist Trude Dothan, provides an excellent example of digging according to a predetermined grid, often consisting of 5-m squares. Unexcavated walls known as balks both separate the squares and form sections which are carefully photographed and drawn. The history of all the squares can then be correlated to achieve an overview of the whole site.

to the landscape archaeologist and excavations can be very limited in extent.

Other techniques new to archaeology have also recently been introduced. Demographic surveys in different parts of Israel have produced estimates of average carrying capacity of the land of 100 people per acre (25 people per dunam). The renewed interest in ethnography (the use of parallels from social anthropology) has also helped in the interpretation of archaeological data, for example in agriculture. In other words, simple but technical descriptions of objects by archaeologists have given way to the interpretation of their function, using parallels with societies that have been scientifically studied by anthropologists.

Methods of excavation

When excavating a large tell with city walls of different periods, one traditional method is to cut a trench through the defences from top to bottom. The result resembles a cake with a neatly cut parallel-sided slice removed from it. By careful examination of the sides of the trench, the archaeologist can see all the different phases of the city's defensive systems. Objects such as pottery, metalwork and coins help to date the structures.

Trenching can be extended to examine the site as a whole, and at one time this was the accepted method of excavating a tell. Although it may not reveal the complete plan of any single building, this technique does provide a view of the whole history of the site and material relating to each period of its use. Most archaeologists, however, also want to retrieve the architecture and overall plan of the site, as well as a historical sequence, so they then dig in squares according to a predetermined grid. Within each square the walls, floors, pits and any other feature can be examined, before digging deeper. A combination of a trench through the defences to obtain an overall sequence, and a detailed examination of other areas excavated in squares, is now the approach adopted on most large, multi-period sites.

Dating methods

Another question archaeologists regularly have to answer is 'how old is this?'. Modern dating techniques, such as radiocarbon (Carbon 14) dating and tree-ring dating (dendrochronology) are now widely used. Samples are sent to laboratories for analysis, but the results are known only after digging has finished for the season. The archaeologist, however, also needs

A standard typological sequence such as this for pottery oil lamps is a useful tool for dating the different levels in an excavation. Here the main shapes in use between the late 3rd millennium BC *and the mid-1st millennium* AD *are shown. The lamp develops from a simple, round, saucer shape in the Early Bronze Age to an increasingly closed shape. The four-spouted lamps of EBIV are very characteristic of the period.*

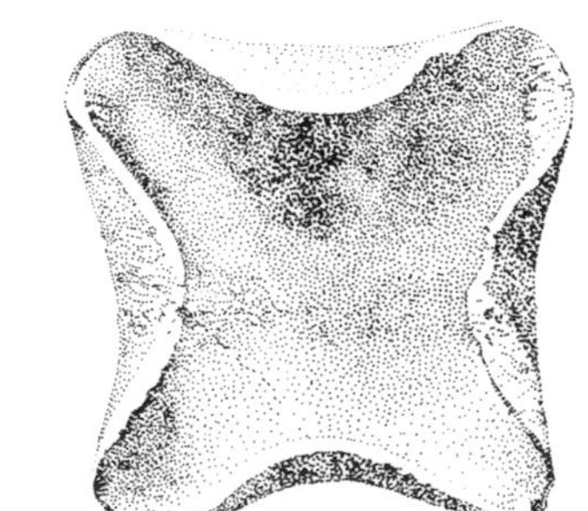

Early Bronze IV

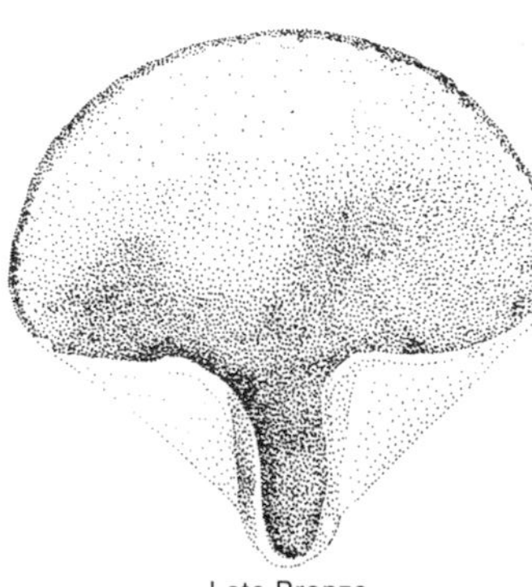

Late Bronze

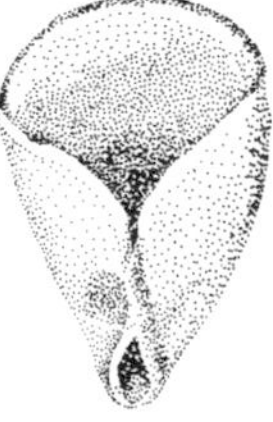

Hellenistic

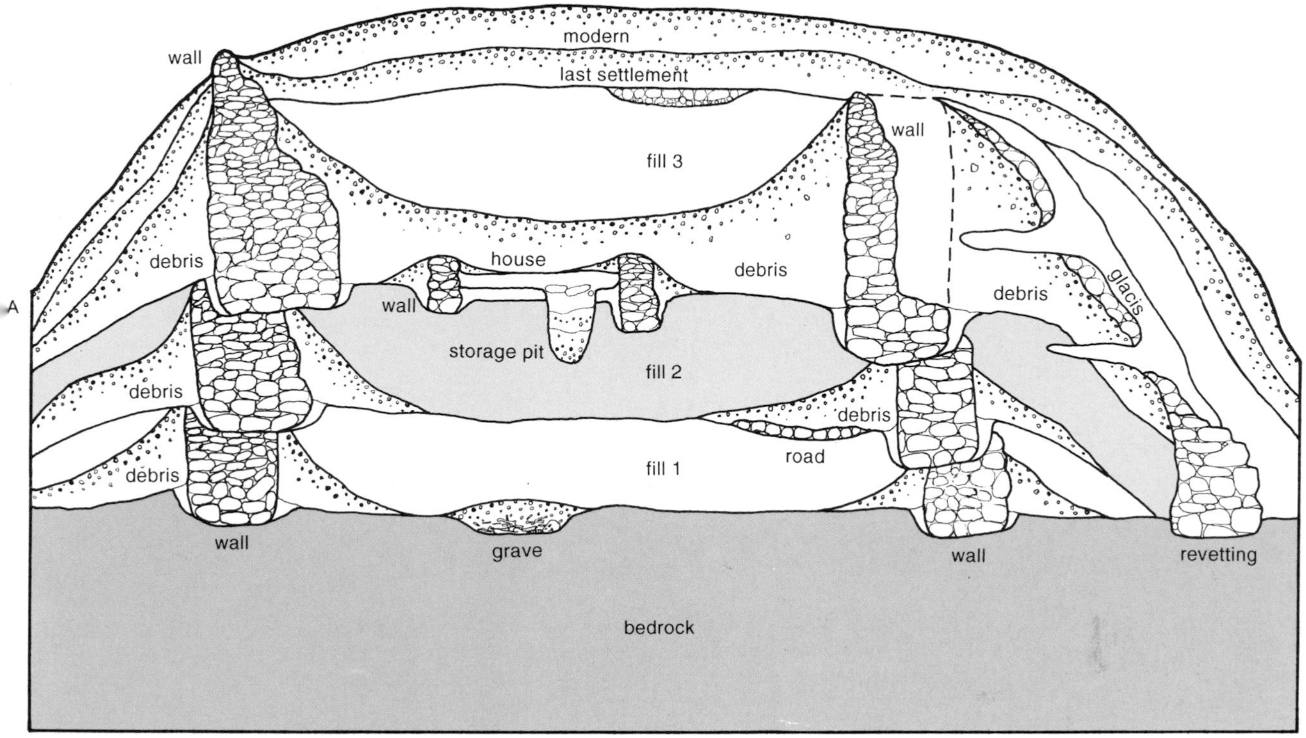

an immediate answer to the question of date while digging is still in progress. Dating finds in the field still relies on stratigraphy and typology, as it has always done.

Stratigraphy is based on the geological principle that superimposed layers form a chronological sequence – so each layer is later than the one below it. In archaeological sites there may be, for example, floors of different periods laid one on top of another, and those finds which can definitely be associated with each floor probably belong to the time it was in use.

Typology is the most useful method for establishing the relative date of finds. To take a modern parallel, many people would be able to assess the approximate date of a motor car from its appearance. In the same way, oil lamps and bronze axes are good examples of ancient objects for which reliable typological series have been established. Whole pots are very rare finds, except in burial caves, but even fragments can be dated if decoration or handles, rims or bases, characteristic of their period, survive.

Assigning a date in calendar years (an absolute date) to an object in the course of an excavation is more complicated. Flinders Petrie (p. 19) was the pioneer who established the historical framework for Palestine. While digging at Tell el-Hesi he was able to date most levels of the mound by imported Egyptian objects found in them, whose dates he knew from his excavations in Egypt. Everything made locally contained in the same levels as the Egyptian objects could then also be dated, as could similar objects found at other sites. This method is called 'cross-dating', and it relies on a known historical framework, worked out reasonably accurately for the Near East in the 19th century AD. This in turn relies mostly on references in ancient documents to astronomical events, such as eclipses of the sun, whose dates are known to astronomers.

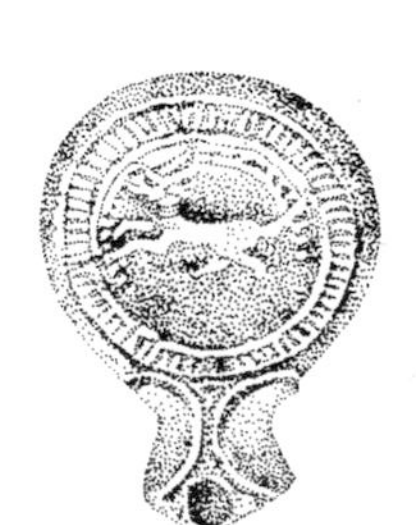

Roman Byzantine

This schematic diagram of an imaginary tell shows how successive walls and the debris of their collapse or destruction build up, forming the mound. The area of building space on its summit decreases as the mound grows higher. Collapsed walls have to be levelled up with a fill to give a reasonably flat surface on which to build new structures. The characteristic steep slopes of the tell were created by the defensive glacis, often laid over boulders and retained by a wall at its foot. 'Horizontal digging' of tells – the stripping of artificial levels – was fashionable between the two world wars. But if this were to be done along the line A–A in this diagram, a mixture of material from several different periods would result, making a correct interpretation of the site almost impossible. It has now been universally recognized that it is essential to dig according to the real levels of each site.

The Origins of the Alphabet

ϹΙΜΩΝΠΕ ΘΩΜΑϹΟΛ ΝΟϹΛΙΛΥΜ

GREEK
Official and monumental Greek inscriptions always used capital letters, while the cursive script ('handwriting') was used less formally. The first Greek Bible manuscripts, like the one above, were written in capital letters called 'uncials'. From the 7th century AD *manuscripts were written in small cursive letters called minuscules, from which derive the script you are reading in this book today.*

וְשָׂרַי אֵשֶׁת אַבְרָם

HEBREW
The vowels are shown by the addition of dots and dashes above and below the line. The method in use today is that developed by the Massoretes in Palestine in the 1st millennium AD *(p. 29). Hebrew was no longer spoken by that time, but it remained the holy language of the Law, read aloud each week in synagogues. It was therefore important to know how to read it properly and thus a vocalization system was needed.*

ARABIC
Because the prohibition against the graven image has always been so strong in Islam, the written word has become one of the great inspirations for Moslem artistic creativity. Arabic, like Hebrew, has a vowel system which can be added above or below the words. It also has, to a much greater degree than Hebrew, a system of diacritical marks – these tell the reader how to distinguish between letters that look similar.

The Phoenicians who came [to Greece] with Cadmus [Prince of Tyre] introduced into Greece a number of accomplishments of which the most important was writing, an art until then, I think, unknown to the Greeks.
Herodotus, *The Histories*, V, 58

LITERACY – READING AND WRITING – is one sign of an advanced society. True writing began in Mesopotamia about 3300 BC and the concept (though not the writing system itself) spread to Egypt very soon thereafter. In both lands the writing method was syllabic, that is, one in which each sign stands for a consonant, often with a vowel sound attached to it, or sometimes a consonant – vowel – consonant. A scribe often needed to learn hundreds of signs before he (or occasionally she) could read and write fluently. Alphabetic writing represents a great advance on Mesopotamian cuneiform or Egyptian hieroglyphic, because on the whole it is far simpler to learn and to use. Wherever syllabic systems were used, literacy tended to be limited to a very few; most rulers were unable to read or write for themselves and always had scribes beside them, even for their personal correspondence. In the places where alphabets were the rule, literacy could and did become widespread. Although scribes were always employed by a majority of the population to read or write letters, many people in the Levant were lettered by the later 1st millennium BC.

The original Canaanite alphabet, from which all Semitic and later European alphabets are derived, had 22 letters. Each sign stands for one single sound rather than a group of sounds. Only consonants are represented. In fact Semitic languages such as Hebrew, Aramaic and Arabic are still generally written without any vowels, although in relatively recent times vowel systems have been added to the script, by the addition of dots and dashes above or below the line of writing.

The notion of alphabetic writing may have arisen twice on the soil of the Levant. The Late Bronze Age scribes of Ugarit wrote in an alphabetic script with new symbols, modelled on the cuneiform principle of wedges stabbed into soft clay, sometime between 1400 and 1200 BC. A small clay tablet discovered at the site bears the 30 letters of their cuneiform alphabet in its correct order, not unlike the order we have today.

Semitic letter names and their English meaning and sound	*Proto-Sinaitic, 15th century* BC	*Proto- or early Canaanite 13th century* BC	*Phoenician 9th century* BC	*Classical Greek capitals and letter names*
aleph (ox)				A alpha
kaf (hand) k				K kappa
maym (water) m				M mu
'ayin (eye) '				O omicron
ros (head) r				P rho
sin (tooth) sh				Σ sigma

The tablet was probably a teaching text. Although texts using this script have been found as far afield as northern Canaan, dating to the same period and later, this cuneiform alphabet, along with several like it at Byblos and various other places, eventually came to a dead end.

The early Canaanite alphabet

The real precursor of modern alphabets was already in existence by the time of the Ugaritic version. As far as we know, it had developed out of the hieroglyphic script of Egypt from as early as the 17th century BC. This could have happened in Canaan, or in Sinai, where the Egyptians were mining for turquoise at Serabit el-Khadem, in the western part of the peninsula. Local people, of the same Semitic background as the population of Canaan, worked alongside them. When the Egyptians dedicated a shrine to their goddess, Hathor, the 'locals' were quick to emulate them. They made little figurines of human-headed sphinxes or seated scribes in the Egyptian fashion, and inscribed them with the name of their goddess. When these statuettes were first found at the beginning of the 20th century, the short group of letters was a total mystery. Subsequently Sir Alan Gardiner believed that the signs had been taken from the Egyptian hieroglyphic script and treated as if they were pictures of objects; but the objects had been named by the Semitic miners in their own language. Thus the picture of a house was called in Canaanite 'bayit'. And then, just as an English-speaking child today would say 'H is for House', so the miners said, 'B is for Bayit' – and the alphabet was born. Some scholars call this script Proto-Sinaitic, but others point out that it is also known from short inscriptions in Canaan from this same period (the Middle Bronze Age), and that therefore Early Canaanite is a better name.

The Early Canaanite alphabetic script was so simple that it was used increasingly over the next centuries in a variety of ways: to mark personal possessions such as arrowheads (for easy retrieval from the battlefield); to dedicate offerings in shrines (such as the Lachish ewer; see p. 52); or to keep official records. None of these records have survived, however, since they were written on papyrus or vellum which would have perished in the humid climate of the Levant. Only cuneiform texts inscribed on clay tablets, such as the Amarna Letters – diplomatic correspondence from the time of the Pharaoh Akhenaten (p. 55) – have come down to us.

LE BALAAT INSCRIPTION
This inscription, found on several figurines from Sinai, sometimes written left to right and sometimes right to left, was the key to the decipherment of Early Canaanite. The inscription reads 'le Balaat', meaning 'for the goddess', showing that the figurine is a votive gift to 'the Lady', who was the female equivalent of Baal.

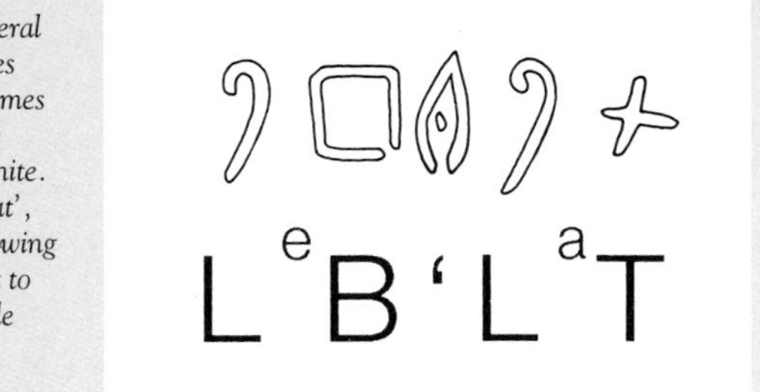

The Phoenicians

The earliest known monumental alphabetic inscription carved on stone is on the lid of the sarcophagus of Ahiram, King of Byblos, dating to the 11th century BC. The script had become more regular and had assumed its classical form and from this time on it is usually referred to as Phoenician. Evidence for alphabetic inscriptions before the 1st millennium BC is mostly limited to the southern Levant and it is quite possible that the classic form evolved there; but there is no proof for this at present.

During the 1st millennium BC the Phoenician alphabet spread northwards through Syria and Turkey and westwards to Cyprus. It also travelled with the Phoenicians to their new Punic colonies along the north coast of Africa. However, by the time Carthage and other Punic cities were founded the alphabet had already arrived in the west via the Greeks.

Inscriptions and the Bible

Several inscriptions throw direct light on the narrative of the Old Testament. Among these are the House of David inscription (p. 83), the Balaam text from Tell Deir 'Alla (p. 20–21), the Mesha Stela (p. 28), Hezekiah's inscription from the Siloam Tunnel (p. 91) and the Lachish Letters (pp. 21 and 91). Other textual finds help recreate the atmosphere of the biblical world, for instance the Gezer Calendar (p. 35) and the tomb inscription of Shebna from Siloam, which mentions his concubine. Small inscribed objects include personal seals in a variety of stones, which sometimes bear a design or a device, in addition to the owner's name. If the person held an official position, the title is given in addition to their name. Seals of members of the royal family are also identified as such, for instance that of Jezebel. Other seals belonged to private persons who are otherwise unknown.

The seal of Jezebel – a grey stone seal belonging to the queen whose name is a byword for wickedness. Most of the royal motifs are Egyptian in origin, such as the winged sphinx and the falcon and cobras forming the symbol known as the uraeus. 1 Kings 16, 31 tells us that Jezebel was the daughter of the Phoenician king of Sidon and it is the Phoenician form of her name that appears on her seal.

The Stela of Mesha, King of Moab, recording his victory over an alliance of Israel, Judah and Edom, referred to in 2 Kings 3, 27 (p. 85). The inscription, in the elegant script of the 9th century BC, *is in Moabite, a language closely akin to Hebrew and Canaanite.*

OSTRACA

An ostracon (pl. ostraca) is a pottery sherd which has been written on (p. 97). In the ancient Near East sherds were used as a form of scrap paper, for quick notes, lists, short letters or file copies. It was a form of recycling old mate rial and saved on the cost of using expensive papyrus. It is fortunate for us that this custom was in use, as papyrus deteriorates quickly in damp climates but potsherds are nearly indestructible. Inscribed sherds have been found in many countries and they add enormously to our knowledge.

The alphabet abroad

By the 8th century BC it is clear from the numbers of ostraca (pieces of broken pottery bearing inscriptions) and other marked objects that literacy was on the increase in the Levant. But this was also the time when mercantile contacts with the outside world were developing very fast. It cannot be a coincidence that the mid-8th century BC is precisely the time when alphabetic inscriptions are found for the first time in Greece. The earliest is on a jug from Athens, which seems to have been offered as the prize in a foot race. The Greeks adopted the names of the letters along with their shapes (so, for example, *aleph* becomes *alpha* and *beth* becomes *beta*) and eventually passed them down to us. Greek belongs to the Indo-European family of languages and the Greeks also added five new letters (*upsilon, phi, xi, psi* and *omega*) at the end of their alphabet for Greek sounds which did not exist in Semitic tongues. To the Greeks also belongs the credit for the invention of the vowel system. With a stroke of genius that seems obvious only in retrospect, they took as vowel signs the Semitic symbols for sounds which had no equivalent in Greek. At first they wrote right to left, in Semitic fashion, or sometimes *boustrophedon*, that is 'as the ox ploughs' – right to left for the first line, then left to right and so on. Eventually the convention was fixed from left to right and the shapes of the letters stabilized into the forms more or less as they are today.

The last element in the transmission of the alphabet into the script you are reading now, took place when the Greeks founded colonies in Italy. The alphabet was taken up by the peoples there, notably the Etruscans, and has come down to us via the Romans, who added a few more letters (C for example) and abandoned some of the Greek ones. In northern Europe in the Middle Ages further refinements were made, including, for instance, the letter W. But ultimately the origin of virtually all the alphabetic systems in use in the world today goes back to the Canaanites of the 2nd millennium BC. The alphabet stands as one of the world's greatest inventions and perhaps the most important inheritance we have from the ancient Near East. Without it we would not have the Bible, nor the rich traditions of Judaism and Christianity, nor the achievements of Classical philosophy and science. The elaborate script of Arabic, the medium for the Koran and the glories of Islamic culture, is also ultimately dependent on the early alphabet of Bronze Age Canaan.

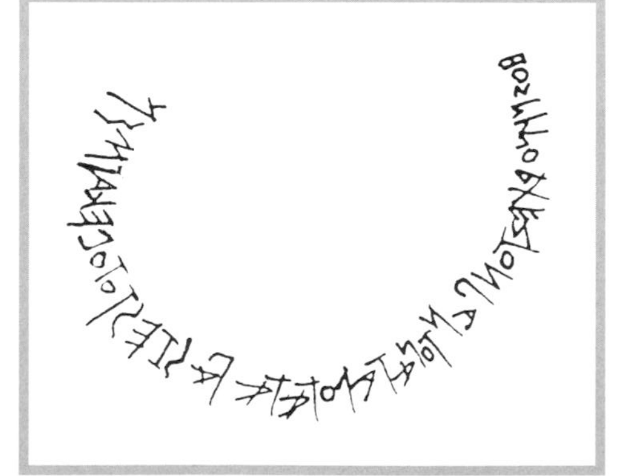

The earliest known Greek inscription, lightly scratched around the neck of an Athenian jug.

Phoenician consonants 9th century BC	*Greek vowels Archaic*	*Greek vowels Classical*
𐤀	A ᐅ	A
𐤄	Ǝ	E
𐤉	I	I
𐤏	O	O
𐤅	U	Y

WRITING THE BIBLE

Take thee a roll of a book and write therein all the words...
Jeremiah 36, 2

THE BIBLE IS DIVIDED into the Old and New Testaments. Jews consider only the former to be authoritative, and generally refer to it as the Hebrew Bible. Christians believe the New Testament, beginning with the ministry of Jesus in the four gospels (Matthew, Mark, Luke and John), to be more important. To Moslems both sections of the Scriptures are theologically valid and the Bible ranks second only to their holy book, the Koran.

Jews are often called 'the People of the Book', but this simple statement begs the question of what exactly is meant by 'the Book'. The easiest aspect of this issue to resolve is that of the changing physical shape of books. In antiquity the works which make up the Bible were written on rolls of papyrus or leather, and not sewn into the form which we today recognize as a book. The words *sefer* (Hebrew), *biblos* (Greek) and *volumen* (Latin) are always translated into English as 'book', but more properly mean 'a writing scroll'. The format of modern books did not come into general use in the Near East until it was adopted by Christians in the 2nd century AD. True books (called in Latin *codex*, plural *codices*) are more economic than scrolls, because both sides of the sheet can be written on. Thus more material can be contained in a single volume. They are also easier to carry around than a scroll. Jews, however, continue to use parchment Scrolls of the Law (the first five books of the Old Testament), at least for public use in synagogues.

Nobody would dispute that the works contained in the Bible cover a vast span of time from the Creation to the days of Jesus and Paul, nor that they were written by many different authors – historians, scribes, poets, prophets, apostles and even kings. Many authorities would also agree that even within a single biblical text there is evidence that many hands were at work at different times. But it is only within the last few decades that many people have come to understand that standardization of the text of the whole Bible is a relatively recent phenomenon. The realization has come about with the widespread publicity given to the Dead Sea Scrolls (pp. 122–25). If the biblical text had been standard from the beginning, many of the pieces – some long sections, others merely fragments – which were found in the caves of Qumran would duplicate each other, but instead they preserve variant readings. What is more, all of these readings were evidently felt worthy of preservation. Clearly at this time (between the 2nd century BC and the 1st century AD) there was no such thing as a single standard text of the Bible. It was not until after the destruction of the Second Temple by the Romans in AD 70 that the rabbis at Jamnia (Yavneh) began the lengthy task, not completed until nearly a thousand years later, of establishing the 'correct' version of the Hebrew Bible (p. 161).

The Massoretes and the Hebrew Bible

Although the text of the first five books of the Bible, called in Hebrew the Torah, or 'the Law' was never as fluid as the rest of the Hebrew Bible, none of it stabilized completely until the 10th century AD. By this time not only the text, but also its correct pronunciation had become a problem for Jews because Hebrew had fallen out of use as a spoken language sometime after the Second Jewish Revolt (AD 132–35). Jewish scholars called Massoretes (*massorah* means 'tradition') recorded this dying knowledge by inventing systems of vowel signs, accents and even musical notation to guide those who chanted portions of the Torah aloud during synagogue services. The Massoretic additions were not, however, added to the Torah scrolls themselves, which were too holy to be interfered with in any way, but were included in manuscripts intended for private study.

The Bible in Hebrew

The Massoretes were also involved in the creation of a definitive edition of the Hebrew Bible by the addition of a critical apparatus in the margins of the text itself. The most important Hebrew text is that of the Massorete, Aaron ben Asher, who lived in the 10th century AD in Tiberias, on the shores of the Sea of Galilee. Two early manuscripts in ben Asher's tradition are preserved – the Aleppo Codex and the Leningrad Codex. It was Aaron ben Asher's version of the Hebrew Bible which found favour with Maimonides, the great

PAPYRUS AND PARCHMENT

Papyrus paper is made from the long split stems of the plant, called the bulrush in the Bible, which grows plentifully in the Egyptian delta. Thin parallel strips are laid in water with a second layer placed at right angles over them. As the water evaporates pressure is applied and the two layers become glued together, creating a fabric-like material. In late antiquity it was exported to the Mediterranean world from the Phoenician city of Byblos, the Greek name for Gebal. Byblos in Greek originally meant 'papyrus', but came to mean 'book' and eventually the Bible.

Parchment (a word derived from the city of Pergamon in Asia Minor where there was a library in ancient times rivalling that of Alexandria) was originally made from sheep- or calf-skin, prepared by stretching it while wet and then cleaning it with pumice. Far more durable than papyrus, it became the most widespread material in use before rag paper.

ORIGEN'S HEXAPLA

In Caesarea a Church Father and theologian called Origen (c. AD *185–254) produced the Hexapla which arranged six versions of the Old Testament (four of them in Greek) in parallel columns for easy comparison with the Hebrew of the first column. The second column was a transliteration of the Hebrew text into Greek characters.*

DIVISIONS OF THE BIBLE

THE HEBREW BIBLE
The Hebrew Bible (or Old Testament) is divided differently by Jews and Christians. It has three major sections: 1 Torah – *Genesis, Exodus, Leviticus, Numbers and Deuteronomy – also called 'the Law' (the word means 'instruction').* 2 Neveeim – *the Prophets, which further subdivide into a) the Former Prophets (Joshua, Judges, 1 and 2 Samuel, 1 and 2 Kings) and b) the Latter Prophets (Isaiah, Jeremiah, Ezekiel and the 12 Minor Prophets).* 3 Ketuvim – *the Writings (Chronicles, Ezra, Nehemiah, Job, Psalms, Proverbs, Daniel and the five Megilot (Scrolls) – the Song of Solomon, Ruth, Lamentations, Ecclesiastes and Esther. In Hebrew the Bible is called the Tanach, which is an acronym of the initial letters of the three divisions (with the K pronounced as in 'loch').*

THE CHRISTIAN BIBLE
This is divided into 5 parts: 1 The Gospels – Matthew, Mark, Luke and John. 2 Acts of the Apostles. 3 Letters of Paul. 4 Other letters. 5 Revelation.

The Law
The Former Prophets
The Writings
The Latter Prophets
The Gospels
Letters
Acts / Revelation

The Old Testament

Genesis
Exodus
Leviticus
Numbers
Deuteronomy
Joshua
Judges
Ruth
1 Samuel
2 Samuel
1 Kings
2 Kings
1 Chronicles
2 Chronicles
Ezra
Nehemiah
Esther
Job
Psalms
Proverbs
Ecclesiastes
Song of Solomon
Isaiah
Jeremiah
Lamentations
Ezekiel
Daniel
Hosea
Joel
Amos
Obadiah
Jonah
Micah
Nahum
Habakkuk
Zephaniah
Haggai
Zechariah
Malachi

The New Testament

Matthew
Mark
Luke
John
Acts

Traditionally ascribed to St Paul

Romans
1 Corinthians
2 Corinthians
Galatians
Ephesians
Philippians
Colossians
1 Thessalonians
2 Thessalonians
1 Timothy
2 Timothy
Titus
Philemon
Hebrews

James
1 Peter
2 Peter
1 John
2 John
3 John
Jude
Revelation

The New Testament was originally written in Greek, the lingua franca of the Classical world. Nearly 5,500 manuscripts of the New Testament are known, of which about 2,300 are lectionaries – selections used in Christian services – and only 59 contain the complete New Testament. The earliest fragment found so far is this portion of John 18, written on papyrus and dating to between AD *100 and 150 and now in the John Rylands Library in Manchester, Great Britain.*

The oldest complete New Testament is the Codex Sinaiticus, found during the 19th century AD *in the library of the ancient monastery of Santa Katerina at the foot of Mt Sinai, and now in the British Library. It was written, like its near contemporary, the Codex Vaticanus, on parchment in elegant capital letters called uncials, during the 4th century* AD.

Jewish scholar who lived in Spain in the 12th century AD, and which formed the basis of the great Bomberg Bible, printed in Venice in 1524/5. This became the standard text on which most Hebrew bibles have been based ever since.

The Old Testament in translation

Since it now seems that many versions of the same scriptural material were preserved at Qumran (and also in other ancient libraries), they must all have been considered to have equal validity, preserving different traditions and theological points of view.

The difficulty of maintaining textual accuracy is compounded with problems of translation. All translation inevitably involves interpretation, but many translators of the Bible deliberately went beyond the process of simple translation in order to expound the scriptures in a way appropriate for their own communities. This trend was already apparent in the two Targums (Aramaic) and the Septuagint (Greek), translations made for the Jewish communities of the diaspora in Hellenistic times. Indeed, the Septuagint (p. 113) was originally considered too free by many Jews, although it later came to be venerated almost equally with the Hebrew original. It was quoted extensively in the New Testament and the order of the books in the Septuagint underlies the order of the Christian Old Testament.

The history of the New Testament

For the very earliest Christians the Scriptures still meant the Hebrew Bible, taking from the various versions those readings which best suited their needs. The first truly Christian writings were the letters of Paul to churches around the Eastern Mediterranean. By the middle of the 1st century AD the generation who had witnessed the ministry of Jesus was passing and it was realized that accounts of his life would be needed for the burgeoning Christian communities. Thus oral traditions which had built up about him were gradually collected and written down in Greek, the universal language of the day. Many scholars today think that the gospel according to Mark was the first to be written, and that the accounts in Matthew and Luke depend on it. The gospel of John may be up to a century later in its final form.

The oral and written traditions of the early Christians were as flexible as those of the Jews. Scribal errors and differences of interpretation crept into the texts and, in addition, not all Christian writings were universally accepted among the different communities. The canon of the New Testament was not fixed for the Eastern Church until AD 367 and for the Western Church by the Council of Carthage in AD 397. It took until AD 419 for such works as Hebrews and James to be included in the western canon at the instigation of St Augustine of Hippo. In the west the New Testament now contains 27 works; in some eastern churches the number varies. Among the Copts, for instance, there are 38 canonical books, while for the Nestorians of Syria there are only 22.

Translating the Christian Bible

The work of translating the New Testament from the Greek began very early. By the 2nd century AD there were already versions in at least two languages: Syriac (a Syrian dialect of Aramaic, spoken among remote communities in Lebanon until recently and still used liturgically in the Syrian Orthodox church) and Old Latin. The Latin translations were very fragmentary and frequently became corrupt in the hands of different scribes.

Jerome and the Vulgate

In AD 382 Pope Damasus commissioned Jerome (*c.* AD 185–254) to produce a text of the Bible in Latin which would be standard throughout the Church. Jerome took up residence in Bethlehem and spent the next two decades on this task, producing the version known as the Vulgate, which is still in use in the west, where it underlies many translations into modern languages. Before AD 1000 there were versions of the Bible in the vernacular of most countries with Christian communities, such as Coptic, Ethiopian, Gothic and Arabic. In England as early as the 7th century AD various parts of the Bible were translated and in oral use in the liturgy. The written form came a little later, but it was not until John Wycliffe (c. 1329–84) and the Lollards that the complete Bible was translated into English from the Vulgate.

William Tyndale (c. 1494–1536) is often called the Father of the English Bible. Translating from the Greek version of Erasmus (published in 1516 in Holland), Tyndale's New Testament appeared in 1526. It was the first English version to appear in printed form and is the foundation for the King James Version. He only finished work on the first five books of the Old Testament before he was burned at the stake as a heretic, for trying to bring the Bible within reach of ordinary people.

Official sanction was finally given for a translation into English in the reign of James I. A committee of 54 scholars worked for six years before the King James, or Authorized, Version appeared in England in 1611. The invention of printing with movable type brought the Scriptures within reach of more people. The first printed Bible – the Gutenberg Bible – was published in Latin around 1455. In Europe over 100 editions of the Vulgate alone appeared before 1500 and there were numerous vernacular versions too. It is estimated that today the Bible has been translated into about 2,000 different languages in over 300 versions.

No man was so rude a scholar but that he might learn the Gospel according to its simplicity.
John Wycliffe

If God spare my life, ere many years I will cause a boy that driveth the plough shall know more of the scripture than thou dost.
William Tyndale, *when faced with the argument that Christians needed Canon Law (i.e. Church Law) more than God's Law (i.e. the Bible).*

THE TORAH
The Torah (the Scroll of the Law or Five Books of Moses) is the most sacred part of the Jewish scriptures. Orthodox Jews believe that the Torah was dictated by God to Moses on Mt Sinai and is so holy that not one 'jot or tittle' of it may be changed. The scribe (sofer) who writes it must offer special prayers each day before beginning work and uses parchment, ink and reed pens expressly prepared for the purpose. Horizontal lines are lightly inscribed into the parchment and letters are 'hung' from, rather than positioned on them. The individual sheets, each containing several columns of writing, are sewn together with leather thread to make up a complete scroll, which can take up to a year to write.

Plants and Animals of the Bible

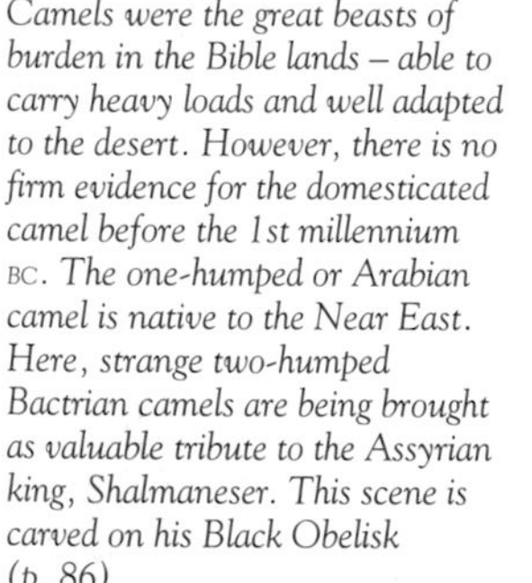

For, lo, the winter is past, the rain is over and gone. The flowers appear on the earth; the time of the singing of birds is come, and the voice of the turtle is heard in our land. The fig tree putteth forth her green figs, and the vines with the tender grape give a good smell.
The Song of Solomon 2, 11–13

For the Lord thy God bringeth thee into a good land, a land of brooks of water, of fountains and depths that spring out of valleys and hills; a land of wheat, and barley, and vines, and fig trees, and pomegranates; a land of oil olive, and honey.
Deuteronomy 8, 7–8

THE LEVANT, THE HEART OF the Bible lands, is a bridge between three continents: Europe, Africa and Asia. In addition to native species of plants and animals, others from all three continents have colonized the Levant, utilizing the great variety of climate, terrain and vegetation which is to be found there.

To the ancient Israelites, Canaan was a land 'flowing with milk and honey' (Exodus 3, 8 and Deuteronomy 26, 15). To the Children of Israel the image this brought to mind was one of forests and rough grazing land, with plentiful pastures for animals and a profusion of wild flowers in winter and spring for the bees. Such a land was suitable for pastoralists, but during all their years of wandering in the wilderness the Israelites dreamed of settling down and becoming farmers once they reached Canaan.

The agricultural harvest taken to the Temple as first-fruits shows that the Israelites did indeed become farmers. Wheat and barley, grapes and figs, olives, pomegranates and dates (probably in fact the source of the honey of the opening quote) were the seven crops which were the main produce in biblical times. Many other crops were grown or gathered of course, but these seven required the most attention. If they failed, famine threatened the people. The crucial time was the period of 50 days between the festivals of Passover and Pentecost (or *Shavuot*), which fall between mid-April and mid-June. The climate of the Levant is so variable from year to year that special prayers for the right combination of rain and warmth were (and are still) offered at this time of the year.

Camels were the great beasts of burden in the Bible lands – able to carry heavy loads and well adapted to the desert. However, there is no firm evidence for the domesticated camel before the 1st millennium BC. *The one-humped or Arabian camel is native to the Near East. Here, strange two-humped Bactrian camels are being brought as valuable tribute to the Assyrian king, Shalmaneser. This scene is carved on his Black Obelisk* (p. 86).

Wind and rain

The north wind brings the rain needed to swell the ripening cereals; but if the temperature rises too early in the season the flowers of the olive trees open too soon and the rain destroys them. The south wind brings warmth and helps to set the fruit of date, grape and pomegranate; but early heat can scorch the ripening wheat and barley. Too much or too little rain or warmth coming at the wrong time brought extreme hardship for the people. Genesis makes clear that the Israelites sometimes had to go to Egypt to buy food: 'for famine was sore in the land of Canaan' (Genesis 47, 4). It has been said that fears about this perilous situation were symbolized, according to Exodus 26, 35, in the Tabernacle in the wilderness. The table for the 12 loaves, one for each of the 12 Tribes of Israel, was placed by the north wall, the quarter of the rain-bearing wind which ripened the wheat; while the seven-branched lamp (*menorah*), which burned pure olive oil, stood at the south, the direction of the warm wind which set the fruit of the olive.

Of hoopoes and hippos

Hoopoes and hippos are two of the more extraordinary creatures of the Bible lands, neither of which were to be eaten according to the rules laid down for the Israelites in Leviticus (11, 9). The hoopoe, with its flamboyant crest, black and white plumage and long beak for grubbing insects out of crevices, is one of the most spectacular birds of the region. The hippopotamus, most scholars agree, is the animal referred to as '*behemot*' in Job 40, 15. It is one of several biblical animals that no longer exist in the region. The Bible texts are also full of more mundane animals, some very familiar, and important, such as sheep, goat, cattle and pig (this last being forbidden food). Among other domestic animals were donkeys, camels and horses, used for traction and as beasts of burden. Chickens were also kept, though they were introduced quite late. Perhaps the earliest mention of them is in the New Testament, as the cock whose crowing marks Peter's betrayal of Jesus.

Sheep (left) were central to the existence of people in biblical times. They provided meat, milk and wool for clothing, as well as being the primary animal offered in sacrifices. Tending the flocks was such an important part of life that the shepherd and his sheep were used as images throughout the Bible to illustrate God's relationship with his people. One of the chief predators of the flocks was the lion (above). Common in Old Testament times, it had become rarer by New Testament days and is now extinct in the region. This lioness and her cub are depicted in a mosaic from a synagogue in Gaza, dating to the early 6th century AD.

The pomegranate (left) ripens towards the end of summer. This exotic-looking fruit has a bright red juicy flesh with numerous seeds, making it a symbol of fertility. It was often used as a decorative motif: for instance, it was embroidered on the hem of the high priest's robe (Exodus 28, 33–4) and ornamented the pillars of Solomon's temple (1 Kings 7, 20).

Many wild animals would have been familiar sights to the inhabitants of the region, such as the wild ass or onager. The ibex, sometimes wrongly translated as 'wild goat', can still be seen today at such places as Ein Gedi, where they delicately browse on the sparse greenery of seemingly sheer cliffs. In the same area there are still conies (the rock hyrax) and leopards, just as there were in biblical days. Other dangerous animals named in the Bible include wolves and lions, and there were scavengers like hyaenas and jackals.

Birds of all kinds abounded and even today huge flocks stream through the Levant corridor on their migrations between Africa and Europe. Some were hunted for food – the best known is the tiny quail which paused in the Israelite camp on its spring migration and was gathered up and eaten with the manna (Exodus 16, 13). Another migrant is the stork, the 'pious bird', which is still a familiar visitor in spring and autumn. Other birds include varieties of eagle, owls, hawks and vultures, as well as doves and partridges, and water birds such as cormorants, pelicans and bitterns. And there was never a lack of the insects that prey on humans, such as fleas and lice, nor of pests like locusts, hornets, scorpions, asps and vipers.

HEARTH AND HOME IN OLD TESTAMENT TIMES

THE YAVNEH YAM INSCRIPTION

A message, lightly penned on a potsherd and dating to the late 7th century BC, *is a complaint by a reaper to the governor of the small coastal fortress where it was found. The reaper says that an official had confiscated his garment and demands its immediate return, in accordance with biblical law (Exodus 22, 26–27). The reaper promises then to deliver his grain 'in full', suggesting that he had not done so previously.*

The inscription is interesting, not just for its intrinsic value, but because it shows that even an unlettered man could employ a scribe to write a letter, or, as in this case, a complaint, on his behalf. It also demonstrates that an ordinary peasant was able to find a means of his redressing wrongs in ancient Israelite society.

She seeketh wool, and flax, and worketh willingly with her hands. She is like the merchants' ships; she bringeth her food from afar. She riseth while it is yet night, and giveth meat to her household, and a portion to her maidens. She considereth a field, and buyeth it: with the fruit of her hands she planteth a vineyard... She perceiveth that her merchandise is good: her candle goeth out not by night. She layeth her hands to the spindle, and her hands hold the distaff.

Proverbs 31, 13–19

THERE WERE FEW TOWNS of any size in the kingdom in the days of David (10th century BC). Not many were as large as Jerusalem, which, in truth, was very small by today's standards. When large tell sites have been investigated they usually prove to be royal administrative and military centres, like Megiddo, Lachish or Beersheba, in which any ordinary houses were probably those of the military garrison. Recent regional surveys have suggested that the majority of the population lived in small settlements dependent on the nearest large centre for protection and refuge when necessary. The household probably consisted of parents and children with grandparents and other members of the extended family.

Domestic housing seems to have been of a reasonably high standard, though it could be argued that only solidly-built structures would survive for archaeologists to find. The houses were built of mud brick on stone foundations and needed a great deal of maintenance to keep them weatherproof. A similar building plan was followed all over the country – often called the 'four-roomed house', though some examples had only three rooms at ground-floor level while others had more than four.

The rôle of women

Women were mostly concerned with the care of their families and the running of their homes. Whether a wife, concubine or slave – and all three might live together under one roof at this time – a woman's domestic duties were roughly the same, the only difference being in her position in the family pecking-

THE FOUR-ROOMED HOUSE *The typical Israelite house was the four-roomed house, reconstructed below and, on the right, rebuilt at Tell Qasileh. Most domestic activities took place in the central courtyard, either at ground level or on the first floor if the central area was roofed over. Access to the upper floor was by a staircase of wood or stone, with perhaps another from outside the house, as in Ahiel's House in Jerusalem. The rooms were mostly used for storage, except in bad weather or for nursing the sick and for women giving birth. The courtyard and roof of a house thus formed its combined kitchen, eating and living areas and even bedroom, as is still the case today in many countries in the Near East. From the roof of his hilltop palace, David had a view of Bathsheba, his future queen, washing herself in the open air, presumably on the roof of her house, suitably screened from the gaze of her neighbours, but easily visible from above.*

order (Genesis 21, 9–21). Within the family a woman's daily work included fetching water, grinding flour, cooking and looking after children and animals.

Women and girls were also engaged in carding and spinning wool and weaving cloth for family use. The simpler household pots may have been made by women, as in parts of the eastern Mediterranean today, though standardization of pottery types in the First Temple period implies that pots were manufactured in central workshops (Jeremiah 18, 1–2). Women sometimes worked in the fields alongside the men (as in the story of Ruth) and tended the flocks. They also found employment as cooks and bakers in the homes of the wealthy (1 Samuel 8, 13) and acted as midwives, like Shiphrah and Puah in Egypt (Exodus 1, 15).

All women were entirely subject to the men of their family and even though their status was carefully regulated by law, the unfortunate lot of a widow or orphan was proverbial (1 Kings 17, 10–12). Nevertheless, some women had remarkable strength of character. Examples include Miriam, sister of Aaron and Moses, and Deborah, who was both a judge and the leader who goaded Israel into action against Jabin, the Canaanite king of Hazor (Judges 4). Ruth supported her widowed mother-in-law, Naomi, with great fortitude, and became the ancestress of King David and Jesus according to the gospel of Matthew (Matthew 1).

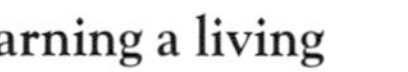

Wool from the sheep or goats was spun using a simple weighted spindle, probably in much the same way as this woman does today, near Jericho (far left). One daily domestic task for the women of the biblical household was baking the bread (centre) that was a staple part of the diet. This pottery figurine of a woman kneading dough on a three-legged table is from a Phoenician cemetery at Achziv, as is that of the woman taking her bath (right) in a shallow oval tub, reminiscent of the story of Bathsheba. Both figurines date to around the 8th century BC.

Earning a living

Biblical society was a feudal pyramid, with the king at its peak and the bulk of the population at its base. Between the two estates were the king's officials in key civil and military posts. They were often the king's relatives, as these were the only people he felt he could trust completely. Priests came from families of the priestly tribe of Levi, whose interests were not always the same as the king's. Professional classes, such as traders, metalworkers, doctors, scribes, and weavers and dyers of fine cloth also found their place in society. The majority of the people, however, were peasant farmers, who grew the crops for food and the flax for making garments and hangings, such as those of the Temple. Then, as now, they were also shepherds and goatherds, whose daily routine was that followed by Jacob when he tended the sheep of Laban, his uncle and father-in-law, in Haran (Genesis 30).

A SCHOOL EXERCISE

The Gezer Calendar, found at Gezer and dated to the late 10th century BC, is scratched into the surface of a soft limestone tablet. The inscription was carved so badly that many scholars think it was a schoolboy's exercise, and this is borne out by the subject matter, which is a mnemonic of the farming year, listed according to the agricultural activity of each season. Several mistakes have been scratched out (for example, the last letter at the left-hand end of the fourth line) and it was scruffily signed with the letters A B I, after which the tablet is now broken. It may have been the name Abijah – and the boy would definitely not have received a good mark for this exercise in penmanship.

II

IN THE BEGINNING

Be fruitful and multiply; a nation and a company of nations shall be of thee and kings shall come out of your loins...
Genesis 35, 11

AROUND THE 10TH MILLENNIUM BC the people of the Near East began the long technological and cultural journey from gathering and hunting to farming and city-dwelling. By the end of the 4th millennium BC the scene was set for the great urban and literate civilizations of Mesopotamia and Egypt. In the northern Levant (modern Syria and Lebanon) people came into close contact with Mesopotamian culture. In the south (Jordan and Israel), the main stimulus came from the Nile valley.

By around 3000 BC the Amorites of northern Syria had spread out from their homeland and were to be found in cities throughout Mesopotamia. They were a Semitic people (Semites are people who speak Semitic languages). Not all Semitic people lived in cities, however. Many preferred a nomadic life, migrating seasonally with their flocks in search of grazing and water. This is the background of Abraham, traditional forefather of Israel. It should be noted that not all scholars think of him as a historical personage.

In the 17th century BC Semitic tribal groups – some perhaps to be equated with the patriarchal clans of the Bible – gained a foothold in the Egyptian delta, establishing their own Hyksos dynasty. They were expelled by the Egyptians in the 16th century BC at the start of the New Kingdom. For the next 350 years the area of Canaan and Syria came under Egyptian control. This was the great cosmopolitan era of the Late Bronze Age. In the eastern Mediterranean trade flourished, with merchants passing between Egypt, the Levant, Cyprus, Crete and Greece. As part of the Egyptian empire, the level of peace and prosperity had never been higher for the people of Canaan.

A detail from the 'Standard of Ur', dating to around the mid-3rd millennium BC and now in the British Museum, showing a Sumerian with a mixed flock of sheep and goats. The motif of the good shepherd with his flock goes back to the most ancient period of Near Eastern history and also stands for the patriarchs –Abraham, Isaac and Jacob – who, with their extended family clans, were pastoralists rather than farmers.

BEFORE THE BIBLE

There were giants in the earth in those days...
Genesis 6, 4

THE CLIMATE OF THE NEAR EAST around 12,000 years ago was as warm as it is now, but rainfall was higher and forests flourished. Over the following centuries, as the ice of the last glaciation melted, sea level rose worldwide and in the eastern Mediterranean archaeologists have found remains of early villages under the sea, off the coast of Israel. Around this time some groups took the first hesitant steps towards producing their own food and tending herds, rather than relying on hunting and gathering.

The Natufians

The Natufian, dating from the very end of the Old Stone Age (Epipalaeolithic, around 10,500 to 8300 BC), is the best known and most widespread local culture in the Levant at this period. It takes its name from a cave in the Wadi en-Natuf in the Judaean Hills where it was first identified.

In addition to caves, the Natufians were the first people to live in permanent villages, of perhaps up to 150 people. They had simple houses, partly dug into the ground, the sides of the pit held in place by stone boulders. Roofs were made either of skin or thatch. Inside, traces of hearths and storage pits for grain and other commodities have been found. The Natufians still lived by gathering and hunting and they made seasonal forays from their home settlements into the drier areas to hunt, mostly for gazelle, then a common animal in the region, which was also often represented in art.

The characteristic stone tools of this period are tiny blades called microliths. These were hafted into bone handles to make composite tools used to cut cereal grasses for food, or cane and straw for roofing, mat-making and basket-weaving. Stone pestles and mortars to grind flour from cereal grasses or nuts or acorns are quite common, while at Eynan near the Sea of Galilee, finds include bone fish-hooks, harpoons and net sinkers.

Burials have been found at many Natufian sites, containing bodies buried on their sides in a contracted (tightly crouched), position. The dead were frequently accompanied by jewellery, often of shell, and other grave goods, such as animals carved from stone and bone.

From food gathering to food producing

Much scholarly debate has focused on the shift of emphasis from food gathering to food production and from a mostly nomadic life to a settled existence. This is the point of transition from the Old Stone Age (or Epipalaeolithic in the case of the Natufians) to the New Stone Age (Neolithic), characterized by farming communities. In the Levant the Neolithic is

THE TOWER OF JERICHO

The settlement at the oasis town of Jericho was excavated in the 1950s by the British archaeologist Kathleen Kenyon (right). In the PPNA the site was already large and was surrounded by a defensive system comprising a dry moat and a high stone wall. Behind the wall was a solid tower (left) built of rough stones coated with a layer of mud plaster, still surviving to an impressive height of 27 ft (8.2 m) with a diameter of 28 ft (8.5 m). Inside, a staircase gives access to the top. Since the tower was inside the wall it was probably not built for defence, but it is hard to find another explanation for it. Whatever its purpose, such a monumental structure at this early period is an astonishing achievement, both architecturally and for the degree of social organization implied in such a large communal public project.

divided into two: the earlier before the invention of pottery (Pre-Pottery Neolithic or PPN) and the latter after it (Pottery Neolithic or PN), dating together to 8300 to 5500 BC.

The Pre-Pottery Neolithic

Several large settlements are known from the first pre-pottery Neolithic period (PPNA), such as Jericho (Tell es-Sultan) in Palestine. With only small variations the culture seems to have been common to the whole region and it was obviously a successful way of life, based on both farming and hunting. While two important cereals, species of barley and wheat, had been domesticated, no animals had yet certainly come under man's control.

Population increased in the following period, PPNB, and large and thriving settlements have been found in various places, such as Tell Abu Hureira on the Middle Euphrates in Syria and the site at Ain Ghazal in Jordan. This covers some 30 acres (12 ha), making it the largest known Neolithic site in the Near East.

Houses were now built with straight walls of adobe or mud bricks on stone foundations. Some had floors of lime plaster, a considerable technological advance, though burning the limestone to produce lime consumed a large amount of timber. Crops, such as emmer and einkorn wheat, barley, peas, lentils and flax were grown. Domestic animals including goats and sheep and, later, pigs and cattle were herded, in preference to hunting. People had become skilled in food production and storage and so settlements could grow to some size.

The invention of pottery

By about 6000 BC many sites, at least in the south of the region, had been abandoned. The reasons for this are not clear, but one theory is that primitive agriculture coupled with tree felling brought about intense erosion. In Syria large settlements continued to flourish, both inland, as at Tell Abu Hureira, and on the coast, such as Byblos and Ras Shamra.

Pottery was invented at this time. At first it was handmade and very crude – the clay used contained large amounts of impurities and firing was poor, with vessels almost certainly baked in the low temperatures of the domestic hearth. Although pottery breaks easily it is virtually indestructible. In the archaeological record it replaces flint implements as the most important means of understanding developments and changes, as well as the differences and interrelationships between various groups.

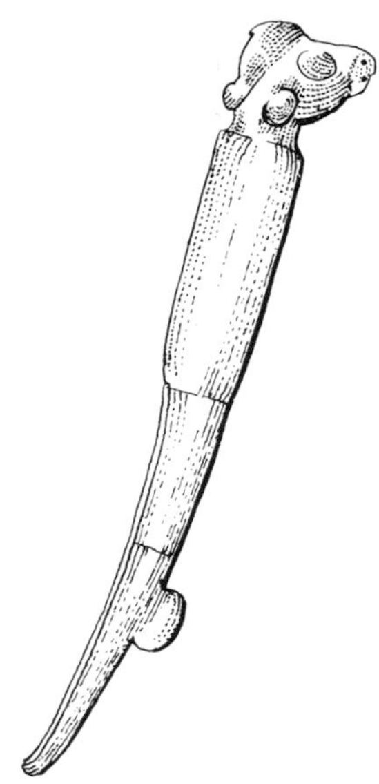

The bone haft of a Natufian knife or sickle, with a representation of a gazelle's head. The delicate carving shows that the Natufians had a developed artistic sense as well as considerable skill. Tiny, sharp bladelets (microliths) of flint were inserted into a groove below the handle and fixed into place with bitumen. When one broke or became blunt, it could easily be replaced.

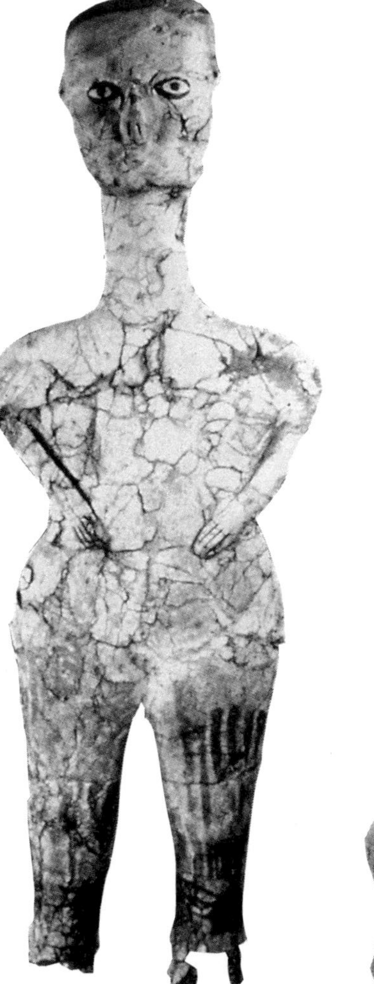

The site of Ain Ghazal in Jordan has been excavated by a joint American–Jordanian team led by Gary Rollefson and Zeidan Kafafi. Towards the end of the 8th millennium BC *Ain Ghazal began as a small settlement of farming hunters. By 6000* BC*, however, it had grown, perhaps containing a population of over 2,000.*

Among the most interesting finds from the site are the extraordinary statues and busts, measuring between 14 and 35 in. (35 and 90 cm) tall and dating to between around 7000 BC *and 6500* BC*. Made of lime plaster modelled on a core of reed and grass, many had painted details in green, red and black. The full figures may represent either men or women and the smaller busts may be of adults also, or possibly children. Over 30 examples have now been found in different caches and they may be evidence of an ancestor cult, like the famous plastered skulls from Jericho, examples of which have also been found at Ain Ghazal. The dead at this time normally had the head removed from the body and buried beneath the floor of a house or in a courtyard.*

Some of the remarkable objects from the Nahal Mishmar treasure, which consisted of over 400 pieces made of copper.

Secondary burial may have been the usual way of disposing of the dead in the Chalcolithic. Once the flesh had decomposed the bones were collected up and put in boxes, or ossuaries, some of which were painted to resemble houses.

Early metalworkers

A great technological leap came in the Levant when people first began to exploit copper in the second half of the 5th millennium BC. The Chalcolithic, as this period is known (*chalcos* is Greek for copper), lasted for most of the 4th millennium. Finds of copper objects are quite rare, probably because the metal was highly valued and broken items would have been recycled.

The number of settlements rose, though oddly many were located in marginal areas. Most houses were of the 'broadroom' type, that is a room broader than it was long. This design was one of the most persistent in Canaan for both domestic and sacred architecture, lasting right through the following Early Bronze Age.

There is little evidence for either public planning or works on any scale. A single large building, possibly a shrine, is the most that has been found at any one site. The small temple complex at Ein Gedi, on a cliff high above the oasis, with magnificent views across the Jordan valley, was not attached to any settlement and may have been a religious centre for various tribes and communities throughout the south.

The Cave of the Treasure

Many of the finds of this period display a high technical and artistic sophistication, exemplified by the remarkable copper objects found at Nahal Mishmar in the Cave of the Treasure. Over 400 copper pieces were found, which were apparently ritual in function, including 'crowns' and 'standards', featuring various animals. All may have been made locally, using the lost-wax technique. Ivory for objects in the same hoard possibly came from Africa, via Egypt, or Syria. Such distant trade connections, even if carried on indirectly by intermediaries, are remarkable for the period. Linen and woollen textiles were also preserved in the dry conditions of the cave. The whole assemblage may have been hidden there for safekeeping during some crisis and Professor David Ussishkin has suggested that they in fact originally came from the shrine at Ein Gedi.

Teleilat Ghassul

One characteristic culture of this period is called the Ghassulian, from the village of Teleilat Ghassul east of the River Jordan where it was first found. The site, which covers some

50 acres (24 ha), lies northeast of the Dead Sea in the foothills of the Jordanian Plateau at about 1,000 ft (300 m) above sea level. It flourished from around the late 5th to almost the end of the 4th millennium BC and was frequently rebuilt following earthquakes. Today the environment around the site is almost desert-like, but in the Chalcolithic it would have been much more hospitable. Date palms and olive groves were cultivated, and in addition people grew cereals and pulses. Thus the classic pattern of eastern Mediterranean agriculture was already established. The bones of domestic animals found in Ghassulian settlements show that the inhabitants kept sheep, goats, cattle and pigs, and perhaps some deer as well.

The Beersheba sites

The Beersheba area in this period was well populated – around 63 sites have been found along the valleys of the Nahal Beersheba and the Nahal Besor. In the vicinity of the modern city of Beersheba three sites appear to be separate sections of a single farming settlement, each also specializing in a different industrial activity. For instance, at Bir Matar there is evidence for copper working and at Bir Safadi an ivory workshop was found. A close resemblance exists between the hoard from the Cave of the Treasure and some objects found at the Beersheba sites.

A rather unusual form of architecture was found at these villages. The inhabitants had carved underground caverns and galleries in the soft rock, though it is not certain whether they lived in them or used them for storage.

The end of the Chalcolithic

Most of the sites of the Ghassulian–Beersheba culture seem to have been abandoned suddenly, around 3300 BC. Of these, many, including Teleilat Ghassul itself, were never reoccupied. Different explanations have been put forward for this disaster. Drought may have caused famines and epidemics in the southern marginal zones; or perhaps the Egyptians, at the dawn of the Dynastic period, attacked, forcing the population to flee. It is also possible that immigrants from Syria or Mesopotamia merged with the local people in the north, and formed the Early Bronze Age population there.

The first cities

The Early Bronze Age in the southern Levant spans the millennium roughly between 3300 and 2300 BC. Conventionally it is divided into three main phases, EB I to III, with an additional final phase that differs considerably from all the preceding ones. The earliest phase, EBI

Carved ivory figurines from the Beersheba sites were made to a very high standard, perhaps in the workshop found at Bir Safadi. This male figurine is very worn and measures 13 in. (33 cm) high. The holes around the head were probably to take tufts of hair for a beard.

THE CHALCOLITHIC OF THE GOLAN

Recently a variation on the basic Chalcolithic material culture of southern Canaan has come to light on the Golan Heights, east of the Sea of Galilee. The discovery is largely due to the work of Claire Epstein, who has pursued research in the region over many years. She has located about 24 village sites of the Chalcolithic in the area of the central Golan. Many were quite large, with between 15 and 40 broadroom houses, some of which measured as much as 50 by 20 ft (15 by 6 m). The local basalt rock was used in their construction and for the roughly paved floors. Internal partitions made roofing easier in an area without tall trees.

A unique feature of villages such as Rasm Harbush and Ain el-Harari is that the houses are joined to each other by their short walls and arranged in several parallel rows, with an open space between them, down a hill slope. Doors are generally in the southern, downhill, long wall, with a step down to the floor of the house. Few houses have courtyards and storage pits are rare, presumably because they are hard to excavate in the basalt. Instead many large pottery storage vessels (pithoi) were found.

Almost every house contained at least one pillar figurine. The one illustrated here is typical, with its beaky nose, beady eyes and lugs instead of ears. Only the small horns on this example are unusual, though by no means unique. Epstein has suggested that the round depression present on the top of each head was used as an offering bowl. The prominent noses, which are such a feature of many Chalcolithic objects throughout Canaan– for instance the ossuary and the ivory figurine also illustrated on this page – may reflect a belief in the nose as the seat of the breath of life, a belief reflected in Genesis 2, 7.

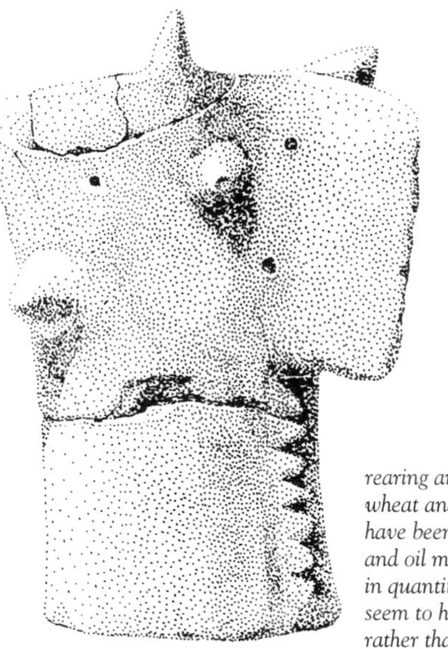

It is not clear whether the villages were occupied year round or only seasonally. The inhabitants practised mixed farming – stock rearing and raising crops such as wheat and pulses. Olives seem to have been the most common crop, and oil must have been produced in quantity. The villages finally seem to have been abandoned rather than destroyed, because the houses had been emptied of all their portable contents. Possibly a prolonged drought forced the people to move elsewhere.

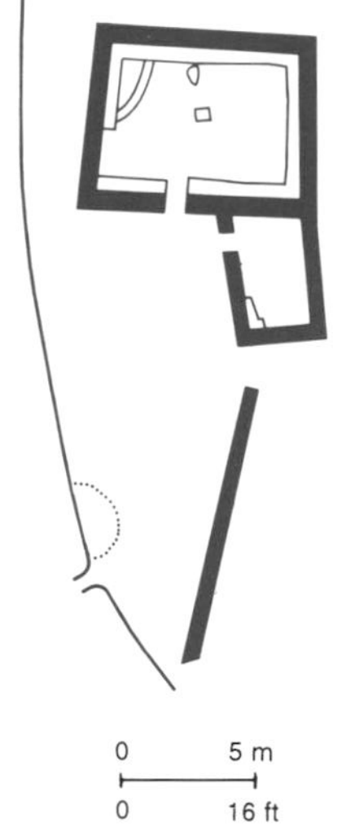

House plans (above) from Teleilat Ghassul (upper) and Early Bronze Age Arad (lower). The single broadroom unit, with the door in one of the long walls, lasted to the end of the Early Bronze Age for both domestic and cultic buildings.

(*c.* 3300 to 3050 BC), was, for the most part, still characterized by farming villages. Many of these settlements were founded at new sites rather than at abandoned Chalcolithic ones and several contained houses of oval plan.

Few sites reached any size. One exception was Arad, in the northern Negev – a large settlement built in a bowl created by the slopes of two hills. This location had the advantage of making the most of the rare rainfall, which ran off the slopes to be caught in a large artificial pool at the lowest point of the town. Arad was a fortified settlement and remains of semicircular defensive towers in the line of the walls have been excavated. Jericho also had a strong defensive system at this time. Social organization had thus developed sufficiently for sizeable communal public works to be undertaken.

The growth of cities

It was only in EBII (*c.* 3050–2700 BC) that urbanism became a significant feature of society in the Canaanite region. This coincides with the emergence of the fully literate urban societies of Sumer, in southern Mesopotamia, and Early Dynastic Egypt. Trade between these powers was growing and many settlements in the Levant were well located to take advantage of the land routes along which trade caravans travelled.

The stimulus for the evolution of cities in the Levant may have come from Egypt, which apart from trade may also have been in contact with the area through colonization or conquest, or alternatively from Mesopotamia, via Syria. Perhaps the impetus was different in the north and south. Sumerian influence was certainly felt in Syria, where the archives of the city of Ebla are beginning to show the extent of that city's commercial links (pp. 46–47).

Megiddo, Beth Shean, Ta'anach and many other settlements developed into urban centres at this time. By modern Near Eastern standards, however, the cities were very small, covering a few acres only. It has been estimated that the total urban area of Canaan in EBII was some 1,500 acres (600 ha), divided between 20 city states, each of which had a hinterland of smaller towns and villages under its control. No one city appears to have been dominant. A standard estimate for the population density of the Bronze Age Levant is 100 persons per acre. This would make the total of urban inhabitants of Canaan in EBII approximately 150,000.

Jordan in the Early Bronze Age is not yet well known, but surface surveys indicate some large cities, for instance Jawa, out in the eastern desert, and Bab edh-Dhra at the southeastern end of the Dead Sea. Neither of these areas could support a large population today and

Aerial view of Arad (right). The Early Bronze Age city is on the left, with its restored defensive wall and semicircular towers. At the lowest (central) point of the site is the reservoir, and, high on the hill, is the Iron Age fortress with its tiny, but important, shrine.

archaeologists believe that they benefited from more rain and a higher water table.

Some cities, both in north and south Canaan, were deserted by the end of EBII. Many different reasons have been advanced for this, including drought, war, epidemics and the failure of trade. Others, however, continued to flourish until the end of EBIII and they presumably absorbed some of the refugees from the abandoned settlements.

The next phase, EBIII (*c.* 2700–2300 BC), was a troubled time. Many cities were attacked, partly destroyed and rebuilt, some several times. This violence may have been the result of rivalry between the cities rather than outside attack. Perhaps nomadic herders (the forerunners of modern Bedouin) could have been responsible for the some of the destructions; others, as before, may have been due to the Egyptians. One side of the Egyptian Narmer Palette (named after the pharaoh it depicts) shows a vanquished Asiatic lying beside a town with semicircular towers like those of Arad.

Decreasing rainfall and soil erosion brought about by deforestation and primitive agriculture may well have led to disputes between cities over prized agricultural land and good water supplies. Fire finally destroyed EBIII Jericho but not all cities met such a violent end. Archaeologists have found that many others declined gradually and were eventually abandoned without any signs of destruction. At Megiddo, partial occupation of the site continued after the end of EBIII.

The collapse of urbanism

By the end of EBIII urban society in Canaan had entirely collapsed. This dramatic change has sometimes been explained as a result of circumstances elsewhere. Egypt had suffered a temporary decline and the trade that was behind the rise of many Levantine cities must have been disrupted. Another theory suggests that the population of Canaan abandoned the cities and returned to a more nomadic life, perhaps as a result of climate change and soil erosion. Social organization was probably based on the extended family or clan system. Several technological innovations took place at this time – tin was combined with copper to achieve the first true bronze and complex moulds for making metal objects were introduced. For the first time the fast wheel was used in pottery making.

Further north on the Syrian coast, the cities of Ras Shamra and Byblos continued to flourish. Inland, however, the story was different; cities there suffered the same fate as those further south and the population was sparse. A few villages in eastern Jordan seem to have had permanent or seasonal settlement: at Bab edh-Dhra the urban site shows no signs of decline. In the Judaean Hills remains of hamlets on the hillsides have recently been discovered beneath the agricultural terraces of later ages.

A detail from the Narmer Palette, a ceremonial slate object which depicts victorious scenes from the reign of Narmer, one of the earliest Egyptian pharaohs. Two dead 'Asiatics' (the Egyptian name for the population of the Levant) are shown. Yigael Yadin has theorized that they represent the peoples of the desert and the cultivated lands. The rectangular shape by the left-hand man may be a schematic representation of a city wall with defensive towers like those at Arad; while the 'key-hole' by the figure on the right is perhaps a trap laid out in the desert into which hunters drove game before killing them. Hundreds of such features can be seen from the air in the deserts of Arabia and Jordan, some of them very large.

Cemeteries and burials

We have more information about people in death than in life, as the widespread and often large cemeteries are better known than settlements. Unlike the previous and following periods, people were generally buried alone, rather than in family graves. Tombs often took the form of shaft graves, hollowed out of the rock, with a chamber opening from the bottom of the shaft. Most burials are secondary with the bones deposited in disarray – the remains may have been brought to tribal centres for interment long after they had decomposed. Grave goods were few and practical; this was not a wealthy society. Men sometimes had a dagger placed with them, while women were given a few beads. Graves often contain some pottery; one of the commonest vessels is the four-spouted lamp (p. 24), very characteristic of the period. Perhaps the lamps were left burning with the dead to light their way to the next world. Jonathan Tubb of the British Museum has shown that these lamps used fish oil, perhaps more easily available than olive oil, and needed the four wicks to burn properly.

ABRAHAM THE PATRIARCH

TENSION BETWEEN CAMP AND CITY

And it came to pass on the third day...that two of the sons of Jacob, Simeon and Levi, Dinah's brethren, took each man his sword, and came upon the city boldly and slew all the males. And they slew Hamor and Shechem his son with the edge of the sword, and took Dinah out of Shechem's house, and went out. The sons of Jacob came upon the slain, and spoiled the city, because they had defiled their sister. They took their sheep, and their oxen, and their asses, and that which was in the city, and that which was in the field.

Genesis 34, 25–28

A family burial cave at Jericho, dating to the Middle Bronze Age. The skeleton of the last person to die lies on the low stone bier, but when the next is buried all the bones will be scattered around the cave. Skulls and bones of the dead can be seen lying in confusion on the floor of the cave, among pottery, grave goods and other debris.

Now the Lord said unto Abram, Get thee out of thy country and from thy kindred and from thy father's house unto a land that I will shew thee...and into the land of Canaan they came.

Genesis 12, 1, 5

ONE OF THE MOST CONTENTIOUS issues in Bible land studies concerns the figure of Abraham (originally Abram), the traditional forefather of Israel. A generation ago scholars such as W.F. Albright and G.E. Wright believed that archaeology would soon be able to prove the historical truth of the Bible (pp. 20–21). Their counterparts today have reacted against this. Many consider that Abraham is the mythic, but not the real, ancestor of Israel.

A few archaeologists and Bible scholars, however, have breathed new life into the ideas of Albright and Wright. They feel that the general agreement between elements of the biblical narrative and archaeological evidence for the Canaanite Middle Bronze Age is too strong to dismiss, making it difficult to accept Abraham simply as a mythical figure. Yet they accept that it is highly unlikely that evidence for Abraham's individual existence will ever be found. He is thus regarded as the ancestor of one element of the various tribes which later joined forces to become the Israelites. Canaan itself is obviously a recognized entity in the biblical account. References to Canaan in the archives at both Ebla (mid-3rd millennium BC) and Mari (early 2nd millennium BC) show that it was already a known geographical term.

Dating Abraham is another point on which opinions differ. The most radical scholars think he lived at or later than the reign of David (10th century BC). What does seem likely is that the patriarchal narratives of Abraham, Isaac, Jacob and Joseph were preserved orally for centuries before being first written down during the period of David. There must then have been a process of editing which lasted for several centuries until the narratives reached the form in which we now have them. Majority opinion still places Abraham in the Middle Bronze Age – the early 2nd millennium BC.

Archaeology and Abraham

Archaeologists have shown that in the Middle Bronze Age the majority of the Canaanite population once again lived in city-states. Among them, tribal peoples retained a nomadic life, searching for grazing and water for their herds and trading with settled communities.

There are many points of reference between archaeology, historical evidence and the biblical narrative. For instance, excavations in many cemeteries of this period show that it was customary to bury several people in one cave. These may have been members of a single clan who were all buried in the same family tomb, calling to mind the story told in Genesis 23 of Abraham's purchase of the Cave of Machpelah in order to bury his wife Sarah. Abraham was himself buried there, as were many of his descendants. Joseph and his brothers even brought the bones of Jacob, who had died in Egypt, back to the ancestral burial place.

The story of Sinuhe

Texts from Mesopotamia and Egypt have also yielded possible parallels with the way of life described in Genesis. The Middle Bronze Age in Canaan roughly coincides with the rise of the Middle Kingdom in Egypt. A 4,000-year-old text tells how an Egyptian courtier called Sinuhe fled the court of the pharaoh, Sesostris I, and found safety in the tents of a powerful nomadic leader called Ammi-Enshi who seems to have ruled much of inland Syria (an area the Egyptians called Upper Retinu).

Sinuhe married the daughter of the sheikh and was given his own tribal lands to govern. It

A Bedouin household encamped in the desert, such as, perhaps, Abraham and his family would have lived in. This is one of the famous black woollen tents woven on portable looms by the women of the family from the wool of their goats.

was a fertile region, full of cereals, fruit, honey, figs and excellent wine. He owned herds and hunted game. In the years Sinuhe lived with the tribes he played host to many Egyptian travellers, in the best traditions of hospitality witnessed in the patriarchal narratives of Genesis (for instance 18, 1–8). The tale of Sinuhe is reminiscent of the story of Moses in the tents of Jethro (Exodus 2–3), but Sinuhe was eventually pardoned by Sesostris and returned to Egypt, where he wrote his memoirs.

The Semites

Sinuhe calls the man with whom he found refuge an *amu*. The Egyptian word can be translated as 'a Semitic inhabitant of Canaan'. It is language that identifies ethnic affiliation and the Canaanites spoke a Western Semitic language. Many personal names found in the texts in the state archives of Mari (p. 47) and in Egypt were Semitic, and it is generally agreed that Semites were the dominant element in the population of Syria and Canaan at this time.

It is clear from the documents that the people of the region, both settled and nomadic, were all of the same stock. Many, like Sinuhe's patron, were nomads, wandering throughout the whole Levant. These tribes usually had a home base, perhaps focused on a clan burial site. Such bases could be tent encampments or villages, and were often sited near large towns. Relations between city and camp were potentially explosive and one example of conflict is related in Genesis 34 (sidebar). It is quite likely that the settled population could easily turn to this lifestyle if necessary, as Abraham's family had done. The situation in Middle Bronze Age Canaan is therefore often seen as the background to the story of Abraham's wanderings.

THE LIFE OF ABRAHAM

Abraham was born in Ur in southern Mesopotamia, but at the command of the Lord he and his family became pastoralists and first migrated to Haran, in Syria. After the death of Terah, Abraham's father, they moved south to Canaan, where they settled. Mamre (later Hebron), in the southern Judaean Hills, became their tribal centre, when Abraham negotiated the purchase of the cave of the Machpelah in which to bury his wife, Sarah (Genesis 23, 16–20). The clan periodically returned there to bury their dead and perhaps to trade, exchange news and to barter for brides. The importance of a foreigner acquiring such a site was recognized by both parties to the deal. Abraham came to the court of the town, held as was common at the main gate, and presented himself as a humble supplicant and a stranger in the land. He was offered the hospitality that was due and then negotiations began. By his purchase of the property from Ephron, Abraham was not only able to bury his dead, but had acquired a legal stake for his tribe in the land itself. The traditional site of the Machpelah is still venerated in the great mosque in the heart of Hebron, the Arabic name of which remembers Abraham – el-Halil, the friend of God.

CITIES OF THE TIME OF ABRAHAM

And he said, Thy name shall be called no more Jacob, but Israel.
Genesis 32, 28

MANY LARGE, POWERFUL cities flourished in the Near East during the late 3rd and 2nd millennia BC. Some of these must have had an influence on developments in Canaan, if only indirectly. Among the best known are Ur, the city from which Abraham traditionally set out for Canaan, then in southern Mesopotamia (now in Iraq), and Ebla and Mari in Syria.

Ebla

In 1975 archaeologists working at a site in northern Syria called Tell Mardikh discovered an archive of clay tablets, jumbled together in a room of the building they had been stored in. Over 15,000 fragments were found, dating to the 23rd century BC. When deciphered it was found that the texts formed the royal archives of the palace of the ancient city of Ebla.

Part of the palace complex was a large audience courtyard. A throne dais was situated under a shady portico on one side, with two archive rooms along an adjacent wall. When the king held court he could call on scribes to bring him any records he needed from the store. The documents were inscribed on soft clay tablets which fitted comfortably in the hand. They were baked hard, and thus preserved, when the palace burned down.

The palace scribes wrote in cuneiform, the script of Mesopotamia, and used two different languages. One was Sumerian, the most ancient of all the languages of Mesopotamia, and the other was the tongue of Ebla itself, often called 'Eblaite'. This is the oldest Western Semitic language so far discovered.

The contents of the tablets cover all manner of subjects, from economic, commercial and legal concerns, to chronicles of the history of Ebla. There are tablets dealing with the activities of the gods of Ebla, who are also known from the tablets found at Ugarit, which date,

Clay tablets fallen from their shelves in the royal archive at Ebla (above). The destruction of the city by Naram-Sin in the 23rd century BC, later earthquakes and the ravages of time have all contributed to their disarray. Luckily, however, not all the tablets crashed to the floor; some slid gently down, still in the order they were arranged on the wooden shelves – reconstructed right, using the holes preserved in the plaster floor to locate the uprights. The edge of each tablet was marked with its subject and number.

however, to about a thousand years later (p. 52). Collections of hymns, proverbs and rituals as well as other forms of literature were also found among the texts. The Ebla tablets provide a fascinating and remarkable insight into the culture of this sophisticated, literate city-state which flourished between the mid-3rd millennium BC to around 2290/2250 BC when it was destroyed by Naram-Sin of Akkad.

Some spectacular claims were made soon after the decipherment of the contents of the tablets, concerning their relevance to the Bible. For instance, it was maintained that there was a god in Ebla called 'Ya' (the short version of Jehovah) and that one king called Ebrum could be Abraham's ancestor Eber. Following further study many of these assertions have been discounted or modified. While Ebla was not, as was once suggested, in direct contact with the towns of Canaan, it certainly did have trading links with cities to the south-east, including Mari. Interestingly, one personal name in the documents is 'Ishra-il'. It seems that Jacob was not the first man to be called Israel (see opening quote).

Mari

The Amorite city of Mari lies on the middle Euphrates in modern Syria. In the 18th century BC its king, Zimri-Lim, partly rebuilt and enlarged the palace there. Mari had commercial and political ties with the state of Babylon, also Amorite, under its ruler Hammurabi (*c.* 1792–1750). Late in his reign, Hammurabi began a policy of expansion that eventually led to the destruction of Mari. As at Ebla, the conflagration that razed the city and its palace in about 1757 BC helped to preserve the state archives, housed near the royal audience hall. Again as at Ebla, the texts deal with every conceivable subject. They range from matters of state and international commerce, to the annals of the kingdom and the personal correspondence of its royal family.

Two aspects of the Mari archives are important for the study of the Bible. First, documents relating to the international trade of the city, show that Mari's caravans reached at least as far south as northern Canaan – to Hazor and Laish (later Dan) at the sources of the River Jordan. Second, there are many reports of attacks on outlying towns and villages which were under the protection of detachments of troops from Mari. The attackers were herdsmen, tribal people who were essentially of the same Amorite cultural origin as the citizens of Mari. They were therefore of a similar background to the patriarchal groups (pp.44–45). One tribe is named *b'nai yamin*, remarkably similar to Benjamin, though it in fact may simply mean 'southerners'. Other names are also familiar, such as Ishmael, and this emphasizes that these Semitic tribal herders all ultimately shared the same ethnic roots.

This rather stern figure is Ishtup Ilum, a governor of the city of Mari before 2000 BC. *The statue was found in the sanctuary behind the great throne hall of the palace at Mari and was therefore probably a votive figure. Such statues were placed before the image of a deity as a reminder of the donor's existence, as a faithful worshipper, even when not there in person.*

Ur of the Chaldees

The city of Ur in southern Iraq once lay on the River Euphrates, but the course of the river has shifted some 10 miles (16 km) further east since antiquity. As we have seen, the Bible tells how Abraham, with his family, left 'Ur of the Chaldees' on the first part of his journey to Canaan. The Chaldaeans were an Aramaic tribe who only appeared in southern Mesopotamia much later (pp. 96–97). The description must therefore have been a scribal

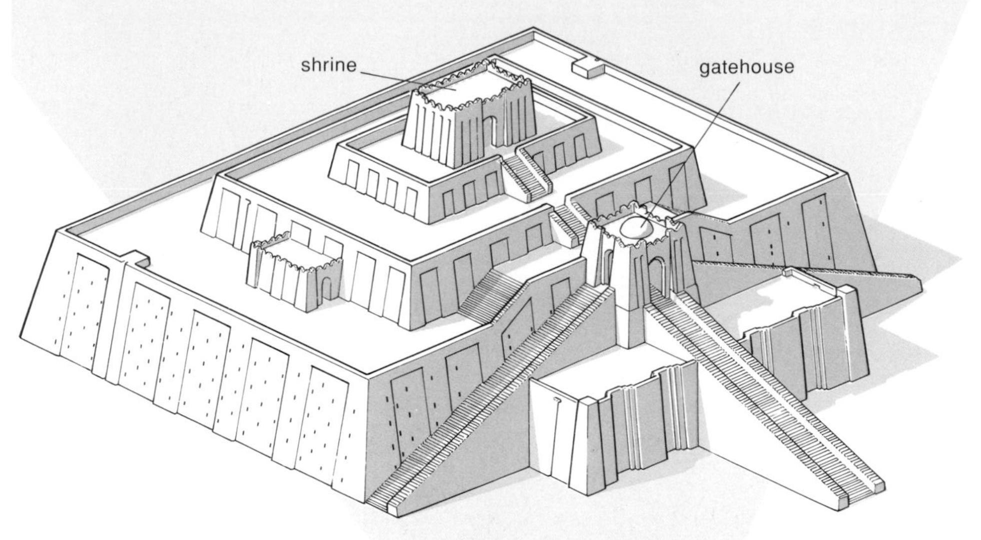

Ur Nammu's restored ziggurat at Ur still stands, with its staircases, to the second of its original three levels. Woolley's meticulous excavations were able to distinguish the different phases of this spectacular building, but unfortunately few traces were found of the uppermost level or the shrine on the top. However, Woolley felt able to reconstruct them as shown here.

The city of Ur (below) maintained its importance through the centuries and buildings were excavated belonging to various phases. The last Neo-Babylonian ruler, Nabonidus (pp. 104–05), held the city in particular regard and rebuilt the ziggurat and several other structures.

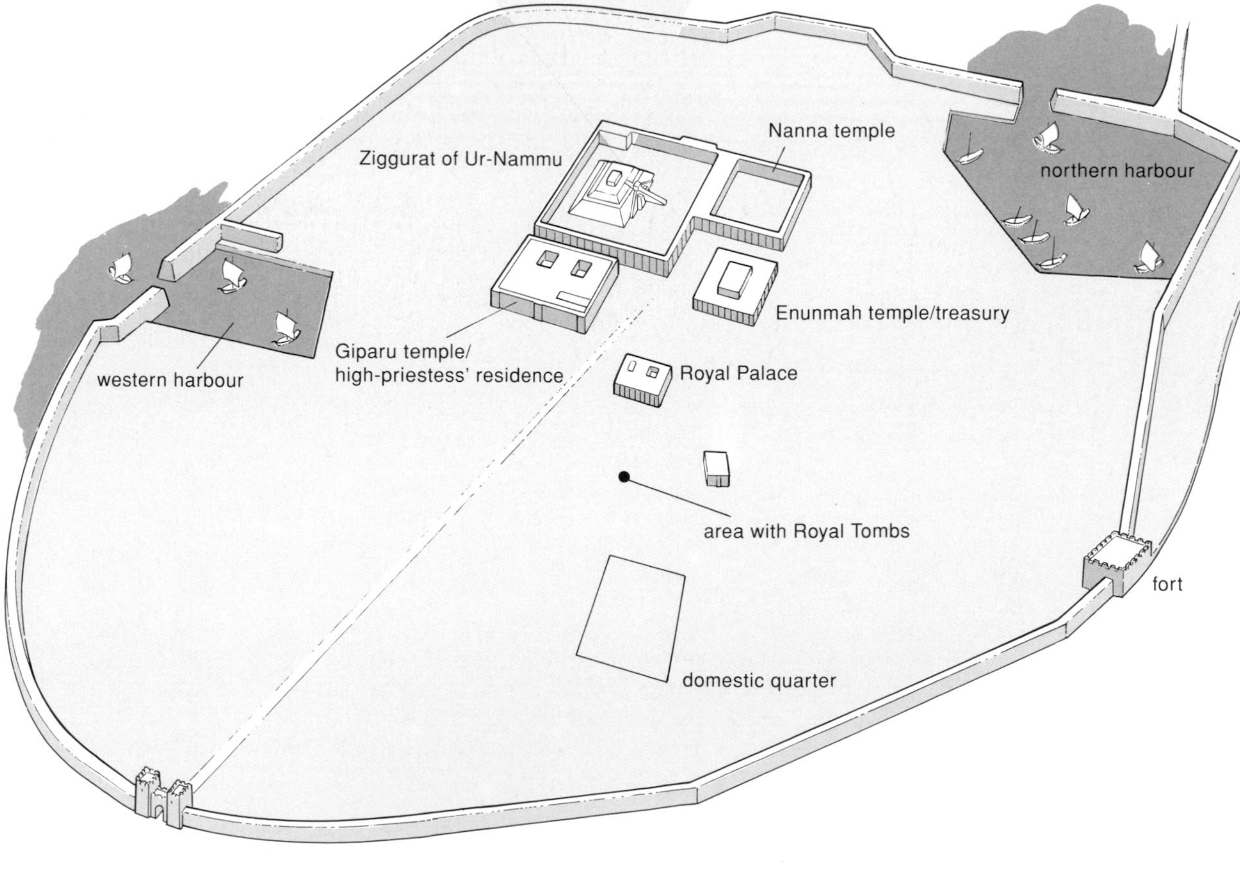

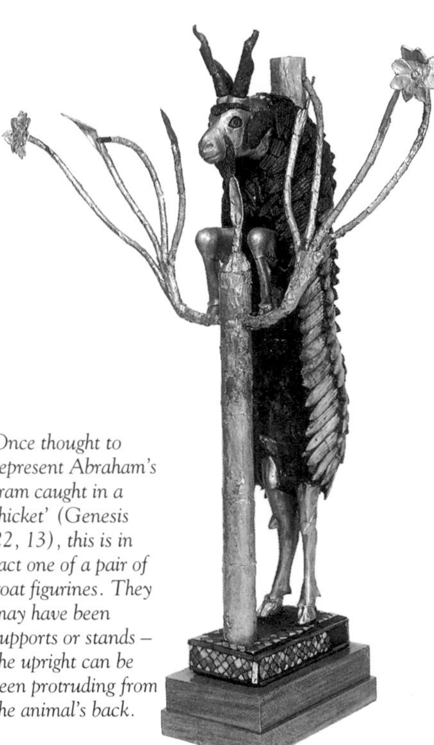

Once thought to represent Abraham's 'ram caught in a thicket' (Genesis 22, 13), this is in fact one of a pair of goat figurines. They may have been supports or stands – the upright can be seen protruding from the animal's back.

gloss to explain the location of Abraham's Ur, written long after the city itself had fallen into ruin.

Ur was one of the earliest and most powerful city-states of Sumer, the southern part of Babylonia. At the very beginning of the 2nd millennium BC, the start of the Middle Bronze Age in Canaan, and the time when Abraham probably set out on his journey, Ur was flourishing and governed other city-states in the region.

Because of its biblical connections, Sir Leonard Woolley (1880–1960) dug at the site as early as 1922. Woolley, along with Flinders Petrie, was one of the first archaeologists working in the Near East to realize the importance of stratigraphy at a site. Of the time he found gold beads from graves in a cemetery at Ur he wrote: 'our object was to get history, not to fill museum cases with miscellaneous curios, and history could not be got unless both we and our men were duly trained.' He thus stopped work on this trench and, despite pleas from his workmen, did not continue excavation there for four years, when he felt sufficiently experienced. When he did return to the spot, in 1926, he uncovered a large cemetery with many simple graves as well as the spectacular Royal Tombs of Ur. These were royal burials dating to around 2500 BC, the contents including gold diadems and other jewellery together with many other beautiful objects.

Much more recently, the texts from Ebla have revealed another town called Ur, somewhere in the vicinity of Ebla. Could this Ur, in northern Syria and near the city of Haran, where Abraham's family made a lengthy stay on their journey to Canaan, be the Ur of the patriarchal narratives? The association with Ur of the Chaldees may be another scribal mistake. We simply do not know.

'WELL OF COURSE, IT'S THE FLOOD!'

When Woolley came upon a deep flood level in one of the trenches at Ur, he was immediately convinced that it was the remains of Noah's Flood described in the Bible (Genesis 7–8). What Woolley had actually found was a deposit of water-laid muds and silts 8 ft (2.5 m) thick, above and below which was clear evidence for human habitation – traces of walls, floors, pits for fires and rubbish dumps containing fragments of pottery, flint and other man-made objects. Woolley believed in the historicity of the Bible – he had come to Ur hoping to find traces of Abraham. It is not surprising then that he quickly arrived at the conclusion that he had found evidence for the Flood.

Woolley's flood dated in reality to about 4000 BC and in fact did not even affect the entire site. Evidence for flood levels of different dates has been found at many sites in southern Iraq since the 1920s. In their lower courses the Tigris and the Euphrates have extensive flood plains, crossed by numerous tributaries and irrigation canals. Rivers such as these flood easily and the water may stand for a long period on the vast plains.

The biblical Flood may be a reflection of the many local inundations that occurred in the low-lying regions of southern Mesopotamia. Or it may contain the distant memory of one widespread, catastrophic event, passed down the generations. The Epic of Gilgamesh is a 7th-century Assyrian version of an earlier myth, possibly dating to the 2nd millennium BC, which mirrors the biblical flood very closely. Perhaps both derive from a common tradition. Modern archaeologists and biblical scholars do point out that the story of a flood covering the entire surface of the land is not very appropriate to the hilly terrain of the Levant and so is unlikely to have originated there.

CANAANITES AND HYKSOS

Hazor, northwest of the Sea of Galilee. In the stable Middle Bronze Age there was not sufficient space on the top of the tell for the increased population, and so they built a huge new lower city at its foot as a suburb. Most of the excavated areas visible in the photograph are remains from the time of Solomon and Ahab, when the site was a royal administrative centre rather than a town.

Now when Jacob saw that there was corn in Egypt, Jacob said unto his sons, Why do ye look upon one another? And he said, behold I have heard that there is corn in Egypt: get you down thither, and buy for us from thence; that we may live and not die. And Joseph's ten brethren went down to buy corn in Egypt.
Genesis 42, 1–3

CITIES WERE ONCE AGAIN built in the Middle Bronze Age (*c.* 2000–1550 BC), some of them on top of the abandoned remains of earlier ones. Traditions of urbanism were obviously preserved during the intervening nomadic era, perhaps in the cities of the northern coast, such as Ras Shamra and Byblos. As is apparent from the archaeological record, these cities continued as large-scale and prosperous settlements with no interruption (p. 43).

Although the impressive defences of many Middle Bronze Age cities argue for a degree of strife, the general picture is one of stability. Together with renewed prosperity went a great increase in population. The period was also one of continued technological developments.

The expansion of cities

The first phase of the Middle Bronze Age (*c.* 2000–1750 BC) was a lengthy period when small unfortified villages gradually grew into large cities, especially along the coasts of Canaan and in the valleys that led inland from them.

By the next period (*c.* 1750–1550 BC) cities were flourishing throughout Syria and Palestine. As they expanded and outgrew their original sites new 'suburbs' were created at the foot of the old tells. At Hazor, in the Galilee area, huge new fortifications were built around 1800 BC to enclose the new Lower Town area. Truly a city, it then covered some 200 acres (80 ha) and may have contained as many as 20,000 inhabitants. It was the most important city of northern Canaan at the time and perhaps held sway over other city-states. The Bible calls it 'the head of all those kingdoms' (Joshua 11, 10). One structure may have been a palace, though its excavator, Yigael Yadin, identified it as a temple. A unique find of this period is the city gate at Tell Dan, the basket arch and barrel-vaulting of which remain intact.

The Execration Texts

Two groups of texts from Egypt tend to corroborate the archaeological information from Canaan. The first texts are written on pottery bowls and date to around 1900 BC; the second are found on figurines made approximately 100 years later. Both sources record curses on the enemies of Egypt in Canaan, hence their name – Execration Texts. The important difference between them is that the earlier texts mention only ten cities by name – Jerusalem is one of them – but there are several instances of regions or tribes with more than one ruler, as might be expected of a partly nomadic society. By contrast, a total of 64 cities, throughout

THE BENI HASSAN FRESCO

The painting from the tomb of Khnumhotep III at Beni Hassan shows a group of Semitic nomads coming to trade in eye-paint in Egypt. They probably also hoped for permission to settle since the whole clan is depicted, complete with baggage, including the lyre one man seems to be playing. The baggage animals are donkeys, rather than camels. There is considerable doubt whether camels were domesticated at this time as no trace of them has been found. Bones of 'equids' (donkeys or horses – it is difficult to tell them apart from their bones) are found in excavations of sites dating to this period in both Canaan and the Semitic Hyksos sites of the northeastern Nile delta, such as Tell Dhaba, now identified as Avaris, the Hyksos capital.

The clothes the travellers are wearing appear to be made of colourful strips which were woven on the narrow, portable Bedouin-type looms and then stitched together. They could be similar to the 'many-coloured', or perhaps striped, coat referred to in the story of Joseph. Joseph's family were given permission to settle in the land of Goshen, the northeastern Nile delta, where there was good pasture for their animals. The Pharaoh – unfortunately not named in the Bible – put them in charge of his own flocks and herds (Genesis 47, 6). This was mutually beneficial: herding was not considered a high-status activity in the Nile valley and the nomadic Semites were excellent pastoralists.

Canaan and Jordan, including Hazor, is named in the second group of texts. Each city has only one king, indicating that this was now a region of city-states and reflecting the increase in urbanization in the intervening years.

Canaanite civilization

An independent Canaanite culture flourished in the early 2nd millennium BC, notable for its technical and artistic achievements, including fine metalwork, especially jewellery, and ivory carving. Egyptian elements, among others, were successfully incorporated into a recognizably Canaanite style. In the Late Bronze Age under Egyptian rule this influence became more direct. The Phoenicians (pp. 66–69) were culturally the heirs of these Bronze Age Canaanite craftsmen. It was they who also perfected the alphabetic system of writing possibly first devised by the Canaanites during the 2nd millennium BC (pp. 26–28).

Rulers of Foreign Lands

Another important source of information concerning Canaan at this time is the tomb of a nobleman and provincial governor called Khnumhotep at Beni Hassan in Middle Egypt, dating to the 19th century BC. The walls of the rock-cut tomb are covered with magical paintings illustrating the life of the dead man. One sequence shows a group of '*amu* of Shut' being presented to Khnumhotep. Their leader is called 'Abisha, ruler of a foreign land'. The Egyptian hieroglyphs may be rendered as *heka hasut* – hence the name by which they are known, Hyksos.

The Hyksos leader's name Abisha is of a Semitic type well known in the Bible. The *amu* constantly mentioned in Egyptian texts from the days of the strong Middle Kingdom and the weak period that followed (the Second Intermediate Period) were, in fact, the inhabitants of Canaan. They were Semites and probably nomadic and tribal, very much like the patriarchal groups of Genesis. Some went to Egypt to trade and others settled there. This fits in well with the story of Joseph's brothers going to Egypt to buy corn at a time of famine in Egypt.

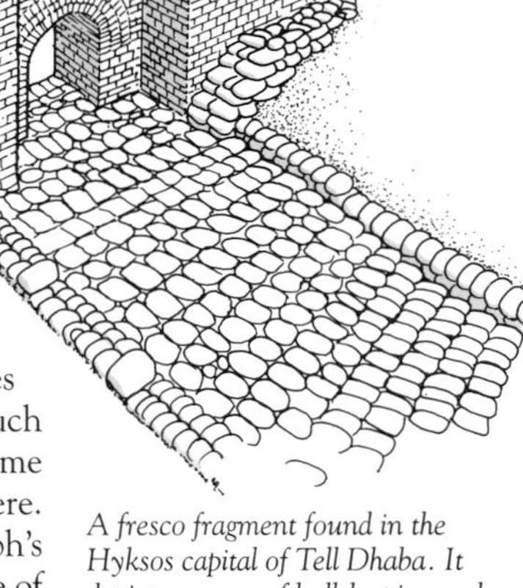

This gate at Dan (right) is unique in that it still stands to its full height and thus shows how such roofs were built. It was luckily preserved when the adjoining defences were raised for safety, by mounding up earth over the gate.

Excavations have shown that many Canaanites made their home in the eastern delta region, called in the Bible 'the land of Goshen'. During the Second Intermediate Period they exerted control over at least that area of Egypt, and possibly parts of the Nile valley as well. This is the Hyksos period in Egypt, which lasted approximately 200 years, between 1750 and 1550 BC. Their centre was at Avaris (Tell Dhaba) where archaeologists have excavated a palatial structure and found evidence for a material culture that is characteristically Canaanite, as well as remarkable Minoan-style frescoes.

A fresco fragment found in the Hyksos capital of Tell Dhaba. It depicts a scene of bull-leaping and in subject and style is wholly Minoan – the culture of Crete.

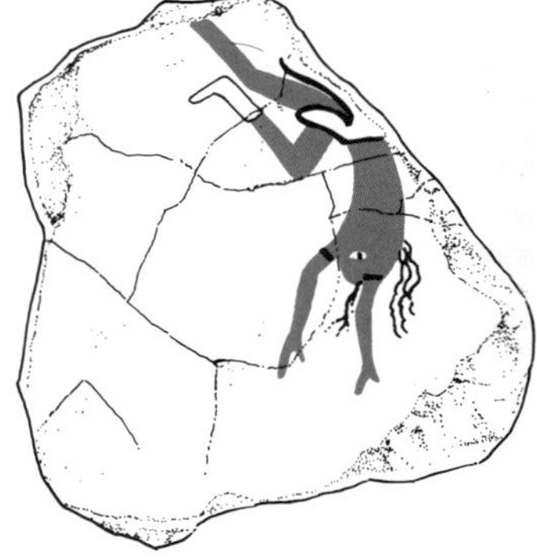

The Gods of Canaan

Stela of Baal, from Ugarit, with the god standing above stylized mountains, brandishing a club and a lance.

And the children of Israel did evil in the sight of the Lord, and forgat the Lord their God, and served Baalim and Asherot.
Judges 3, 7

THE BIBLE MAKES IT CLEAR that the Israelites were to have nothing to do with the gods of Canaan. The very emphasis placed on this prohibition seems to suggest that it was not always observed. This is perhaps not surprising. Israel's god was a stern, ethical being, whose relationship with his followers had been set up by covenants (or treaties) with Abraham, their forefather, and Moses, who led them from captivity in Egypt, and was defined by abstract concepts, such as sin and righteousness. For a people unused to intangible, philosophical ideas, the gods of Canaan, who took human form, were much more approachable and far easier to understand. The Bible singles some of them out by name, in particular Baal and Asherah.

Until early in the 20th century little was known about the Canaanite deities apart from references in the Bible. Then, in 1929, texts were discovered at Ugarit (in north Syria, now known as Ras Shamra). These texts were written in characters rather like cuneiform, but used as an alphabetic system (pp. 26–28) and epigraphers soon deciphered them. Although Ugarit was not in Canaan, the gods mentioned in the texts were the same as the Canaanite ones, and their characters and stories were thus revealed for the first time.

The Canaanite pantheon

The high god of the Canaanites was El, the sky god and ultimate creator of the world. His name is the same as one of the names of Israel's God. El was a rather shadowy figure; the most powerful and venerated figure was his son, Baal. Baal was essentially a weather god, who brought the much-needed rain in the autumn. This was when the New Year began, after the arid heat of summer, when the vegetation had died and the land and its people were parched.

Baal was often depicted in the form of a young man with an upraised arm holding a shaft of lightning or a thunderbolt. Alternatively he was represented in the form of a bull. He was usually worshipped outside on *bamot*, which were either high places or open-air altars. Jehovah, the God of Israel, was also worshipped on *bamot*, but this practice was anathema to the prophets, who tried to stamp it out.

The consort of Baal was Asherah, sometimes also called Elat – the feminine form of El. Another version names Baal's spouse as Astarte. Asherah was associated with the sacred tree – the tree of life, nourishing and fertile, rooted deep in the earth. She is often

A fragment from a Late Bronze Age jug found in the Fosse Temple at Lachish (above). The name of the goddess Elat, Baal's consort, appears above the sacred tree.

Two goats or ibexes flank a sacred tree representing the goddess Elat in this painted sherd from Kuntillet 'Ajrud (below), and an inscription mentioning Yahweh and Asherah.

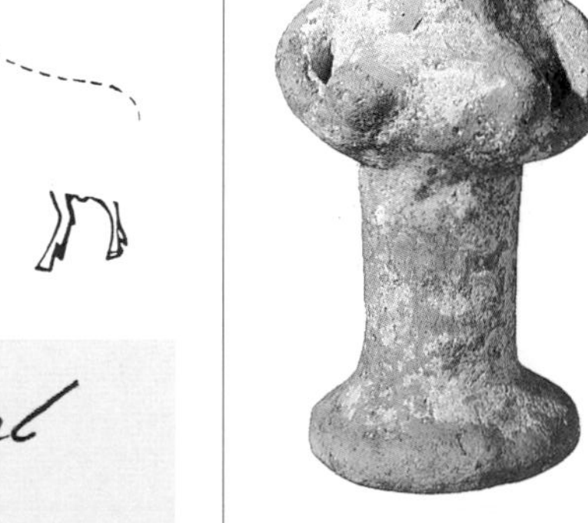

A pillar figurine of the mother goddess (right), smiling benignly. The large numbers and small size of such figurines suggest that they were for domestic use.

depicted as a sacred tree, or with a tree springing from her pubic area. She could also appear as a cow, especially when she becomes confused with her Egyptian counterpart, Hathor. Sometimes, however, she is shown naked and with emphasized genitalia, in a non-Egyptian manner. The Canaanite cults included male and female priest-prostitutes. Intercourse with them was considered an act of worship designed to ensure the fertility of fields, beasts and humankind. These fertility rituals were not incorporated into the ascetic religion of the Israelites, though the fecundity of fields and animals must have been central to their existence. It is understandable then that they sometimes succumbed to the temptations of the gods of Canaan.

'The solitary hill by the water wells'

During the 1980s the small site of Kuntillet 'Ajrud in the northern Sinai desert came to the attention of archaeologists. It is situated on a low hill where three important desert roads meet, and nearby is a rare spring of sweet water. The name means 'the solitary hill by the water wells' and the site must have served as a way-station for travellers over thousands of years. In the 9th to 8th centuries BC it seems that the kings of Israel (then separate from Judah) erected two buildings on the hill, presumably to serve as inns. The better preserved of the two was also a shrine, used by travellers who were devotees of many different gods.

The archaeologists found many pieces of pottery and fragments of wall plaster which have cultic motifs drawn on them or inscriptions, sometimes both. Some mention 'Yahweh of Samaria and his Asherah'. In this context Asherah can only be the consort of the god. We cannot, however, be certain whether this means that some Israelites worshipped Yahweh together with a consort who was called Asherah. This would imply that they were not strict monotheists.

The mother goddess

If Asherah was regarded as the consort of Jehovah by some Israelites in the 8th century BC, her cult was soon suppressed and is not found later. There is certainly evidence for a mother goddess in Canaan at this time, symbolized by the ubiquitous pillar figurines with their large breasts and pleasant smiles. Such figurines may have been among the *terafim*, or household gods, which Rachel smuggled out of Laban's house (sidebar).

The presence of such goddess figurines, as well as Astarte plaques and indeed all sacred images, male or female, poses a problem for modern scholars. It is often not possible to tell from the contexts they were found in whether they were being used by Israelites, Judaeans or Canaanites. Many fragmentary goddess figurines have been found in Jerusalem, dating to the Iron Age.

It is often difficult to disentangle elements of Canaanite beliefs and cult practices from those of early Israel. For instance, the use of stone monoliths, called *matzevot*, for various purposes may have been common to both religions and indeed the two sets of beliefs and customs may have overlapped to a surprising degree.

***Now Rachel had taken the* terafim *and put them in the camel's furniture [saddlebags] and sat upon them. And Laban searched all the tent, but found them not. And she said to her father, Let it not displease my lord that I cannot rise up before thee; for the custom of women is upon me. And he searched, but found not the* terafim.**
Genesis 31, 34–35

A matzevah, *or cult pillar, from the Late Bronze Age Stela Temple, lower city of Hazor – the only one of the set of 10 that was carved.*

Both these plaques (right) depict the fertility goddess. The ears and wigs of both are reminiscent of the cow-eared Egyptian goddess Hathor. The left-hand terracotta plaque shows the goddess in a very un-Egyptian way – naked and full-face. The gold pendant on the right shows her in a more stylized form, with breasts and pubic triangle – with the sacred tree, the tree of life itself, growing out of it.

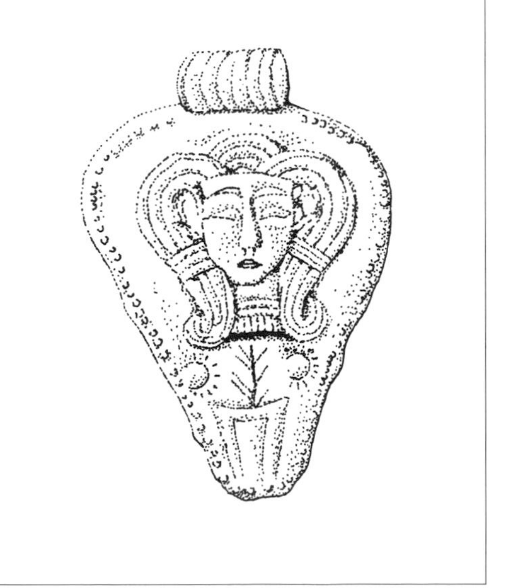

EGYPT'S EMPIRE

And Pharaoh said, Who is the Lord, that I should obey his voice and let Israel go? I know not the Lord, neither will I let Israel go. And they said, The God of the Hebrews hath met with us; let us go, we pray thee, three days' journey into the desert and sacrifice unto the Lord our God.
Exodus 5, 2–3

International trade flourished in the eastern Mediterranean in the Late Bronze Age. The shipwreck discovered off the rocky shore of Anatolia near Ulu Burun provides a glimpse of the prosperity and cosmopolitan interactions of the day. When it sank, the ship was carrying pottery from Greece, Cyprus and the Levant, some of which contained olives, grain, wine and terebinth resin used in making perfume and incense. Ingots of tin from Anatolia and copper from Cyprus were found, as well as bronze tools and weapons, faience and glass objects. Items of precious metals and jewels from Mesopotamia, Egypt, Mycenaean Greece and elsewhere were also included in the cargo.

AROUND 1550 BC, THE PHARAOH Ahmosis (1570–1546 BC) succeeded in expelling the Hyksos from Egypt, marking the end of the Second Intermediate Period. He became the first king of the 18th dynasty, at the beginning of the New Kingdom period. Egyptian records say that the Hyksos were pursued north, into the land of Canaan. This accords well with archaeological evidence, since there are destruction levels at some Canaanite cities at this time, especially in the south. Additionally, an influx of Hurrians, taking refuge from the Hittites, came south and brought a new population element to Canaan. This is reflected by many personal names of Hurrian type found in texts of the Late Bronze Age

The Egyptians consolidated their hold over Canaan during the reign of Tuthmosis III (1504–1450 BC). In about 1490 BC a coalition of 119 rulers from Syria and Canaan came together to face the Egyptians in the valley of Jezreel, but were decisively beaten at the Battle of Megiddo. Tuthmosis proudly recorded the event in the great temple to Amun at Karnak (Thebes), capital of the 18th Dynasty pharaohs. Direct Egyptian rule soon reached as far north as Kadesh on the River Orontes.

Canaan was under the political and cultural domination of Egypt from this point until the end of the Late Bronze Age. The rulers of the once-independent city-states became vassal governors of their own kingdoms, responsible for collecting the tribute and taxation in kind demanded by the Egyptians. However, the Egyptians could not extend their power further to the north because there they came up against the armies of the kingdom of Mitanni.

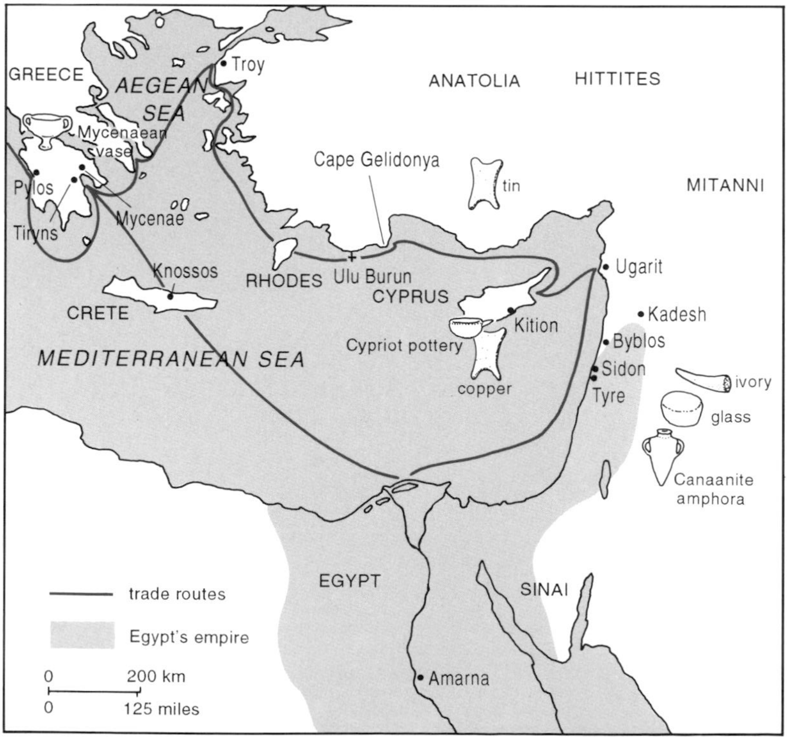

Peace and prosperity

Under Egyptian control Canaan initially experienced a period of enforced calm. Few cities had new fortifications built during the Late Bronze Age. Archaeologists think that at some sites defences of the Middle Bronze Age continued in use, but were allowed to decay gradually. In other places old city walls may have been torn down. At Lachish, in the hills to the south of Jerusalem, a small temple was constructed in the dry moat of the earlier period.

Peace brought with it prosperity, built on international maritime trade with Egypt, Cyprus and the Aegean. One of the great seaports of the day was Ugarit (Ras Shamra) on the north Syrian coast. This city, the capital of a fertile kingdom, was at the centre of a farflung trading network, and was a rich and cosmopolitan place. In the palace, archives were found which shed much light on contemporary Canaanite culture and religion (pp. 52–53).

Cypriot pottery was popular in Canaan and many vessels in a range of styles have been discovered. Pottery also came from Mycenaean Greece, some of it made specifically for the Levantine market.

In the other direction the timber of the Levant was much in demand. Grain, olives and livestock, as well as the famous purple dye of the Levant (p. 66) were also exported. Contacts between Canaan and Egypt were frequent and trade goods passed in both direc-

Amenophis IV – Akhenaten – shown in the strange, elongated but rather delicate style of his day, known from the modern name of his capital city as the Amarna style.

About 380 letters, or parts of letters, on clay tablets have been found at Tell el-Amarna. They were mostly written in Akkadian, which was the Semitic language of Mesopotamia and used as the international language of diplomacy throughout the Near East at the time. Many of the letters were written by scribes in Canaan. From the mistakes they made in writing Akkadian, it is possible to reconstruct something of their own language, which was Canaanite, a Western Semitic language. Very few texts have been found in southern Canaan itself and so this is very important for an understanding of a language that had much in common with Hebrew.

tions. A noticeable Egyptian influence is detectable in the products of Canaan at this period which were still made to a high standard and considered very desirable.

Two shipwrecks found off the southwestern coast of Anatolia, at Ulu Burun and at Cape Gelidonya, provide a graphic record of the extent and richness of the trading links in the Late Bronze Age. The Ulu Burun wreck contained finished objects and raw materials from many different countries. The merchants were almost certainly Canaanite and they must have been trading their way around the coasts of the eastern Mediterranean when they met with disaster. On board were copper 'ox-hide' shaped ingots, probably from Cyprus, Mycenaean pottery, and Egyptian faience, raw ivory and tin. There were objects of gold, bronze swords and jewellery, amphorae for wine, olives and grain. One pithos was found to hold 18 pieces of Cypriot pottery. Some of the items came from beyond the Mediterranean, such as amber beads, which presumably were from the Baltic.

The Amarna period

The first part of the 14th century BC in Egypt was the era of Amenophis IV, who renamed himself Akhenaten (1379–1362 BC). He built an entirely new capital city at Akhetaten – 'Horizon of the Sun [Aten]', known today as Tell el-Amarna. Akhenaten promoted the cult of the sun god, Aten, above all the other gods of Egypt.

The royal archives at Amarna have yielded a tremendous amount of information about conditions in the Egyptian empire and beyond. One part of the archive consists of international correspondence between Egypt and the rulers of other great powers of the time, including Babylon. The records also contain a series of appeals for help from the vassal states of Canaan. It seems that while Egypt was still recognized as overlord of the area, the administrative system set up by Tuthmosis III had weakened. This gave the individual city-states of Canaan the opportunity to attack each other without serious fear of retribution – it was clearly a troubled time.

This little tented shrine was found at Timnah, in the desert of the Aravah, by Beno Rothenberg, who was investigating ancient copper mining in the area. The open-air sanctuary was founded in the reign of Seti I. The head of Hathor is carved on several pillars, so perhaps the shrine was dedicated to her. It was later used by the Midianite miners, who stayed on after the Egyptians had withdrawn in the mid-12th century BC.

Who were the *habiru*?

One name occurs with some frequency in the Amarna letters – the *habiru*. No single translation of the word seems wholly satisfactory, but perhaps the best is 'outsider'. From the letters it seems the *habiru* were social outcasts of various types – bandits preying on law-abiding people. Some were homeless and dispossessed people who formed disruptive elements on the edge of the community. Occasionally the word is also used of foreign workers or mercenary soldiers in the employ of various Canaanite rulers. Labaya, the king of Shechem, in the northern hill country, had so many *habiru* at his command that he was called their chief by his enemies.

A large basalt stela erected by Seti I at Beth Shean to commemorate the Egyptian suppression of a revolt in northern Transjordan. During the reign of Seti, Egypt was trying to re-establish control over Canaan after it had weakened during the Amarna period. Beth Shean was a very strategic site, at the southern end of the Esdraelon valley, guarding the crossings of the River Jordan, and became one of the chief garrisons of the Egyptian army. The site had a long history of occupation and a city flourished there in Byzantine times *(pp. 166–67)*.

Scholars once thought that the *habiru* were the Hebrews of the Old Testament. The *habiru* turn up much further afield than Canaan, however, for they are mentioned in documents from Anatolia, Mesopotamia and Syria from the early 2nd to the late 1st millennia BC. They cannot therefore be identified exclusively with the Hebrews, but the Israelites might have been called *habiru* by others, as for example by Potiphar's wife when speaking of Joseph. Also an Israelite might refer to himself as an 'outsider' when speaking to a non-Israelite (Genesis 39, 14). This may well be how the word 'Hebrew' (the English translation) came to be applied to the Israelites.

Another group mentioned in the Amarna Letters are the *shashu* – the Bedouin who roamed the deserts in every age. They were not directly related to the Israelites, although some tribes, for instance the Midianites and the Kenites, came into close contact with them.

The 19th Dynasty

Under the kings of the 19th Dynasty Egypt regained its firm grip on Canaan. Pharaoh Seti I (1318–1304 BC) built a strong line of fortresses along the route stretching across the north Sinai desert to southern Canaan. These were to safeguard Egyptian control over the area. The route was known to the Egyptians as the 'Ways of Horus' or the 'Nine Days Road'.

Ramesses II (1304–1237 BC) continued the

process of strengthening Egyptian control over its Asiatic empire and was active in the reorganization of the military administration of Canaan. He created strong garrisons at Beth Shean in the north and Gaza in the south. At Deir el-Balah, Aphek and elsewhere, a particular type of building has been identified as an 'Egyptian Governor's Residency'.

The emergence of a powerful Hittite empire in Anatolia was the main threat to Egypt at this time and may have prompted Rameses' strengthening of defences in Canaan. Around 1300 BC a battle was fought between Egypt and the Hittites, under Ramesses II and Muwatallis respectively. This was the Battle of Kadesh, on the River Orontes. Each side claimed victory but in reality it was a draw. The subsequent peace treaty defined the limits of the spheres of influence of the two great powers. However, a new menace was soon to make itself felt and would throw the eastern Mediterranean world into confusion (pp. 62–63). In this upheaval familiar Bronze Age civilizations perished and a new Iron Age world arose.

A gold pendant (above) found in the Ulu Burun wreck, off the shores of Anatolia. It shows a naked goddess, holding a gazelle in each hand. It may have been made in Syria.

A monumental statue of the great pharaoh Ramesses II at the temple of Luxor, Thebes in Egypt. Ramesses was a great builder and it may have been at his new cities in the Nile delta that the Israelites toiled under the oppression of forced labour.

EXODUS AND THE WILDERNESS YEARS

And it came to pass, when Pharaoh had let the people go, that God led them not through the way of the land of the Philistines, although that was near; for God said Lest peradventure the people repent when they see war, and they return to Egypt.
Exodus 13, 17–18

The Greek Orthodox monastery of Santa Katerina in the deserts of south Sinai. Here, at the foot of the mountain of the same name, one of several sites traditionally associated with Moses and the receiving of the Ten Commandments, a monastic settlement was first founded by Queen Helena in the 4th century AD. *It was rebuilt and much expanded over the centuries, and in the 19th century* AD *very important manuscripts were found there, including the famous Codex Sinaiticus (p.30).*

THE EXODUS FROM EGYPT under the leadership of Moses, the wanderings of the Israelite tribes in the deserts of Sinai and their subsequent entry into Canaan are three episodes of great significance in the biblical story of Israel's development. Given the importance of the revelations by God to Moses on Mt Sinai it is likely that some such events did take place at some time, but not necessarily as recorded in the Bible. In the opinion of many historians and theologians the narratives of the Book of Exodus do indeed deal with historical rather than mythical events. The towering figure of Moses stands in relation to the origins of Judaism as does that of Jesus to Christianity. After intensive archaeological research some facts about parts of the Book of Exodus have emerged. Many Hyksos peasantry stayed on in Egypt under their new masters following the expulsion of their leaders (p. 54). They were not slaves, but more like the serfs of medieval Europe, living in their own villages and cultivating their own fields. They were also subject to the strict restraints which the rulers of Egypt laid on all their subjects, native or foreign.

It was the descendants of these people, as well as other resident foreigners and the peasant population of the eastern delta, who were used as forced labour by the Egyptian pharaohs of the 19th Dynasty. The long reign of Ramesses II is particularly associated with massive building projects, especially the new royal residences or capital cities in the eastern delta. These are known to us from the Bible as Pithom (Per Atum) and Raamses (Pi Ramesse). The Israelites set out from the latter place at the beginning of the Exodus and it has been variously identified; the best candidate is a site called Qantir, near Tell Dhaba.

According to the Book of Exodus, Egyptian oppression led the Israelites to pray for deliverance. At the bidding of God, Moses went to the pharaoh to demand the release of the people, but having failed to gain permission, Moses brought down the ten plagues on the Egyptians, culminating in the death of the first-born. The miraculous crossing of the Red (or Reed) Sea (Exodus 14) cannot be linked archaeologically to the drowning of an Egyptian army, though the escape of some fugitive serfs would be too trivial, or too embarrassing, to be mentioned in the annals of Egypt.

Sinai

Once across the Red Sea and out of Egypt proper, the Hebrew tribes were still in the Egyptian dominated territory of Sinai. Four routes cross Sinai towards Canaan. The northern route would have brought them into conflict with Egyptian forces because the line of fortresses existed there. If refugees did ever take that road, and some in fact may have done, it must have been at a period before Seti I's strongholds were built. It is possible that the Exodus recorded in the Bible is an amalgam of ancestral traditions of many groups who were later to make up the historical people of Israel.

Two of the other routes across Sinai traverse the centre of the peninsula, while the fourth skirts the south central massif and roughly follows the coastline southwards, passing Santa Katerina. This is the mountain often identified as the Mt Sinai of the Bible, though there are other candidates, including Jebel Musa a little further north. The Egyptians never penetrated the southern part of the Sinai peninsula and so this route seems the most probable. Jewish tradition does not retain a memory of the site of this most important mountain. Apparently it was not a place of pilgrimage in the early days when the religious beliefs of Israel were bound up with Jerusalem, the Temple and Canaan.

Kadesh Barnea

The Israelites spent many years wandering in the wilderness before their entry into the land of Canaan. One site where they remained for a long time and which archaeologists have sought to identify is Kadesh Barnea, now thought to be the oasis of Ein Qudeirat in northeastern Sinai. This would be an ideal place for wanderers in the desert to stay, since it is an area of lush vegetation and bubbling springs in an otherwise barren environment.

Recent intensive archaeological surveys have explored the whole area of the oasis and have found no evidence for structures predating the period of the Israelite monarchy (10th–6th century BC). The Children of Israel may have lived in tents rather than houses, though some of their occupation debris should have come to light.

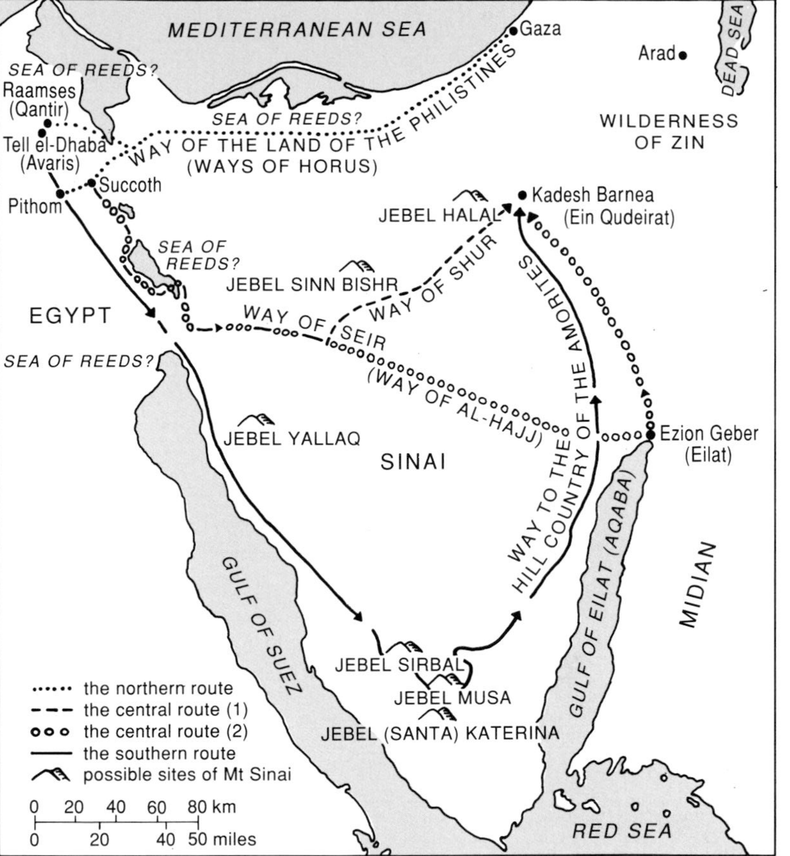

If Ramesses II was the pharaoh of the Exodus, his successor Merneptah was that of the Entry, when, according to the Bible, the Children of Israel were taking possession of the land promised to them by God (pp. 70–71).

Map of Sinai showing the four possible routes by which the Children of Israel could have crossed the peninsula, fleeing from Egypt on their way to the Promised Land.

'ISRAEL'

One piece of historical evidence of crucial importance for dating the presence of Israel in Canaan is the Stela of Year 5 of Merneptah. In his 5th year (1231 BC) Merneptah campaigned throughout Canaan and this stela makes large claims about his successes. Among other victories, he asserts that he has wiped the people of Israel (detail below) off the face of the earth. This is the first known mention of the nation of Israel and demonstrates that the Israelites were a distinct entity in Canaan by that time. Despite Merneptah's claims, though, he obviously did not have such a devastating effect on the nation of Israel.

However, a word of caution is necessary: the stela implies that Israel as a nation is present in Canaan at a date around 1231 BC. This does not help in assessing when they first arrived. It may also refer to a group who already lived in the area, rather than a band newly settled there.

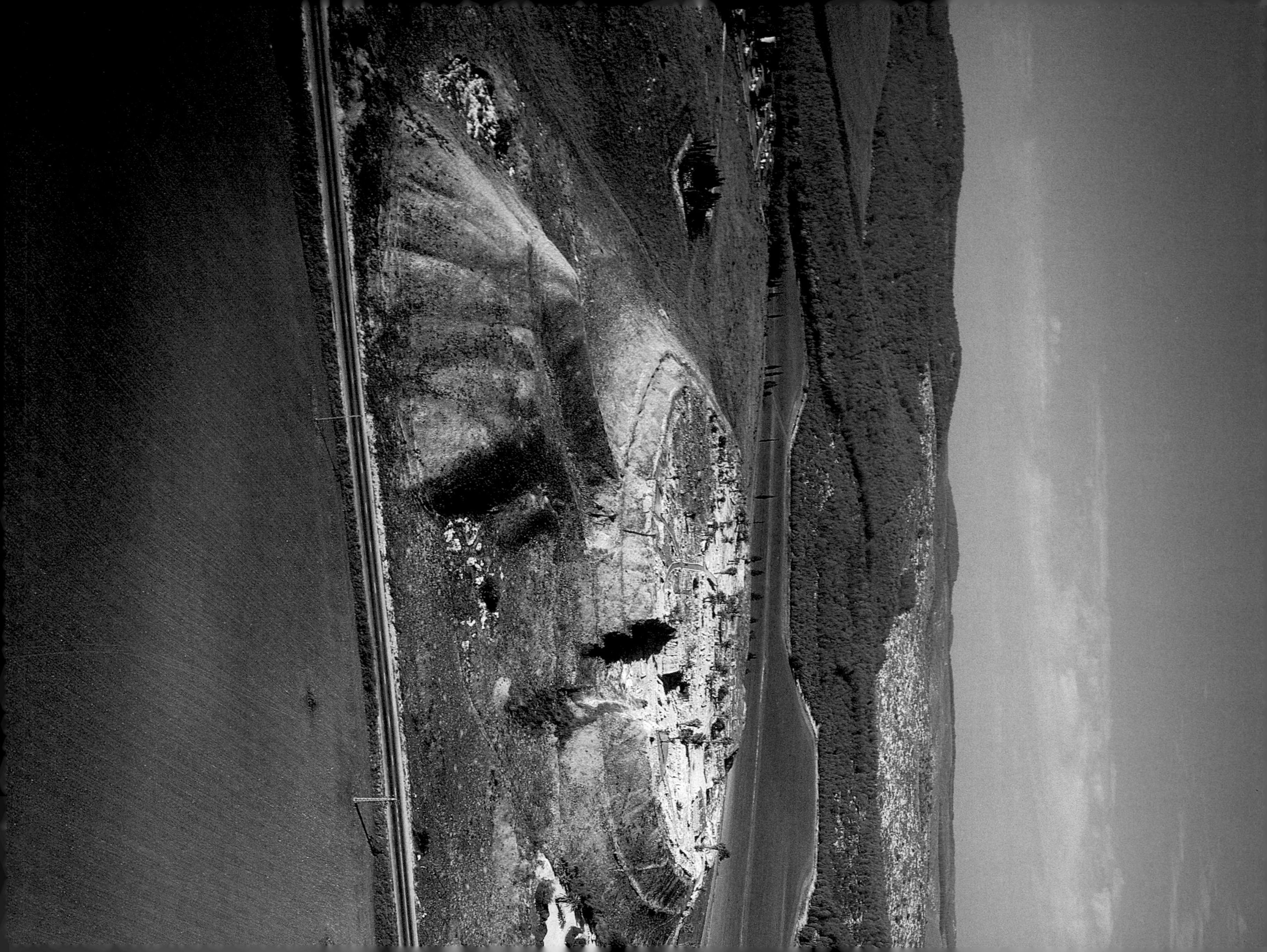

III

OLD TESTAMENT EMPIRES

Judah and Israel were many, as the sand which is by the sea in multitude, eating and drinking, and making merry. And Solomon reigned over all kingdoms from the river unto the land of the Philistines, and unto the border of Egypt: they brought presents, and served Solomon all the days of his life.

1 Kings 4, 20–21

THE 14TH CENTURY BC was a time of peace and plenty in the eastern Mediterranean, its prosperity founded largely on international trade. But all this was to change during the 13th century, for the mighty powers of Egypt and Hittite Anatolia began to decline, Mycenaean civilization in Greece crumbled, the flourishing culture of Cyprus foundered and many of the Canaanite city states were destroyed. The political turbulence disrupted the lives of huge numbers of people, many of whom travelled far from their original homes in search of new land to settle.

The collapse of old regimes signalled great changes for the region, since the stage was now set for the growth of new empires. At first only relatively small groups – such as the Philistines – jostled for position. Soon the classic empires of the Bible established themselves, beginning with the Israelites who created a remarkable empire under King David and his son, Solomon. Later the Assyrians were to achieve supremacy, thanks mainly to the military genius of such leaders as Ashurbanipal. But even Assyrian might was to wane eventually, swept away at the end of the 7th century BC by the increasing power of the Babylonians.

Aerial view of the immense tell of Megiddo. Strategically sited in the valley of Esdraelon, it guards a pass through the Carmel range to the coastal plain beyond. It thus controlled two major international highways, which explains why it was occupied from the 4th millennium BC onwards. Solomon fortified Megiddo and made it one of his administrative centres. Many battles were fought in the vicinity of Megiddo and in apocalyptic imagery it is the site of the battle at the end of days. Armageddon means the hill of Megiddo.

THE SEA PEOPLES

... as for the foreign countries, they made a conspiracy in their islands. All at once the lands were on the move, scattered in war. No country could stand before their arms ... Their league was Peleset, Tjeker, Shekelesh, Denyen and Weshesh...

Inscription at Medinet Habu

FROM AROUND THE 14TH CENTURY BC onwards groups of migrants began to arrive in the eastern Mediterranean. These new arrivals are known to us collectively by one of their Egyptian names as 'The Sea Peoples'. They are perhaps best documented in the Harris papyrus in the British Museum, a source of much information on the reign of the pharaoh Ramesses III (1198–1166 BC). The papyrus preserves the names of individual nations or tribes of Sea Peoples who were particularly active against Egypt. Among them were the Sherden, Weshesh, Denyen, Peleset and Tjekker.

Who were these people, depicted by the Egyptians with their strange headgear, long swords and distinctive round shields? They mostly seem to have originated in the general area of the Aegean and southern Anatolia. The Mycenaean civilization in Greece collapsed towards the end of the 13th century and the eastern Mediterranean powers also fell. It was a time of upheaval and crisis. Whatever the precise cause of these disasters, great movements of population followed, generally migrating from north to south. New groups of refugees were constantly being formed and displacing other peoples in their path.

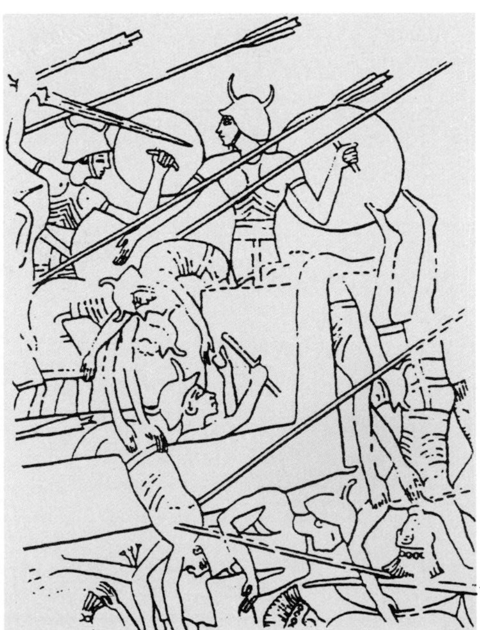

The naval battle between the Sea Peoples and the Egyptian forces under Ramesses III was depicted in reliefs carved on the walls of the pharaoh's mortuary temple at Medinet Habu. Enemy troops are shown wearing horned helmets and fighting with long swords and round shields, identifying them as Sherden.

From trickle to torrent

At first the Sea Peoples arrived in small numbers that could easily be absorbed with by their adoptive countries. Ramesses II (1304–1237 BC) encountered and defeated one group, the Sherden, many of whom were then taken as mercenaries into the Egyptian army and who fought for Egypt against the Hittites at the battle of Kadesh, in about 1300 BC. The anthropoid coffins found at the Egyptian garrisons at Deir el-Balah and Beth Shean in Canaan are possible evidence for the presence of Sea Peoples there. The son and successor of Ramesses II, Merneptah (1236–1223 BC), also had to contend with an attack on Egypt by the Sea Peoples in alliance with the Libyans.

From the later 13th century BC the trickle became an uncontrollable torrent, destroying everything in its path and bringing to an end the long and prosperous era of the Late Bronze Age. This was a time of profound change, which saw the old empires, notably Egypt, lose mastery over the region, and the new order of the Iron Age with its biblical kingdoms emerge.

It was at this point that the Hittites of Asia Minor vanished and the city of Ugarit (Ras Shamra) on the Syrian coast was devastated and never rebuilt. All calls for help sent to Egypt went unanswered. In fact Egypt was itself once again in danger and in the eighth year of his reign (*c.* 1190), Ramesses III fought the Sea Peoples in two battles, one on land and one at sea. A pictorial record of these events, together with an adulatory inscription, is preserved at Ramesses' mortuary temple at Medinet Habu in Western Thebes. The reliefs depict the pharaoh's battles against the invaders in great detail, with various groups being distinguishable by differences in dress and weapons.

The land battle probably took place somewhere in Syria or Phoenicia and the invaders were apparently easily defeated. They are shown on the relief accompanied by their families and all their possessions in the lumbering ox-carts that were carrying them in search of

The lid of an anthropoid coffin from Beth Shean (above). Some scholars have seen in it a similarity to the feathered helmets of the Philistines in the Medinet Habu reliefs. It is certainly likely that some of the Sea Peoples were employed as mercenaries by the Egyptians to garrison their fortresses in Canaan and such coffins may corroborate this. Their odd appearance has earned them the name 'grotesque'.

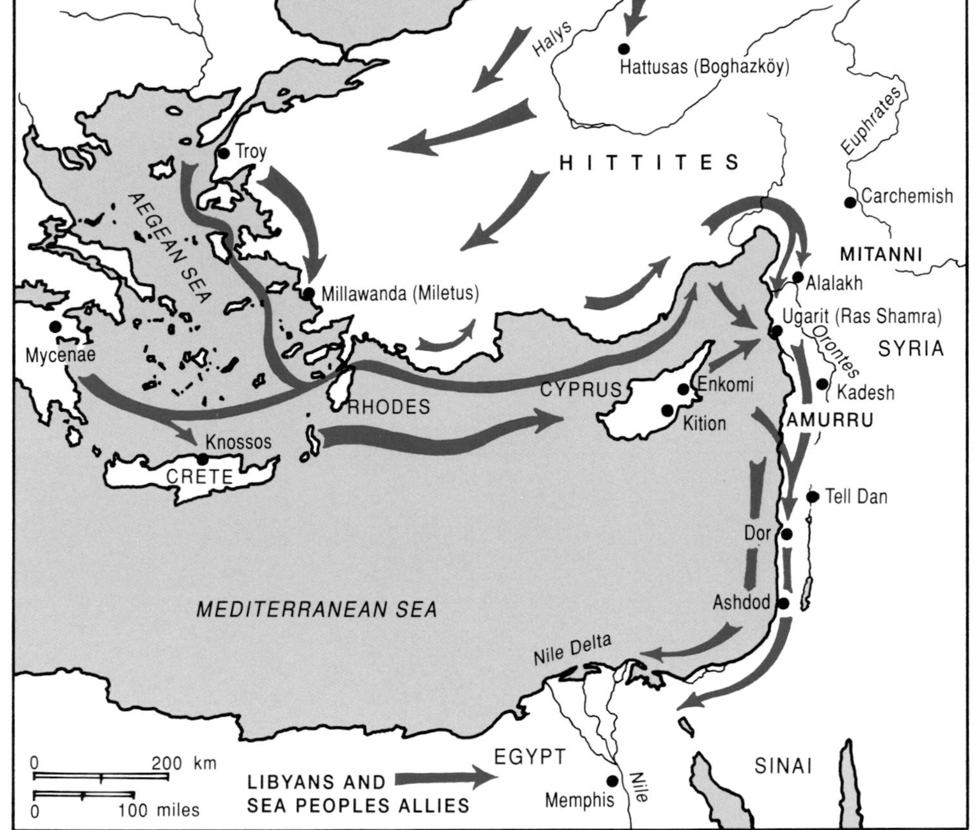

Great movements of peoples took place in the eastern Mediterranean in the Late Bronze Age by land and sea (map, right), causing immense disruption.

new homes. The sea battle was fought in the eastern Nile delta, and this too seems to have been a great victory for the pharaoh.

Ramesses' successes may have averted the threat of an invasion of Egypt itself, but we know from both archaeological and biblical sources that Tjekker and Peleset, and perhaps other Sea Peoples, settled along the coast of Canaan, which, in theory, was controlled by Egypt. The Tjekker settled in the area of Dor, south of Mt Carmel, and the Peleset along the southern coastal area. The influence of the Egyptians in the Levant was declining and as they withdrew the Sea Peoples settled with their families in exactly those areas where they had served as soldiers for the pharaohs.

The name that appears in Egyptian hieroglyphs as 'plst' is transliterated with vowels as 'peleset', rendered in Hebrew as 'plishtim' and becomes Philistines in English. The area of the coast they settled, together with its hinterland, is known to us as Philistia.

One more journey, a linguistic one this time, was undertaken by the Peleset. The Greeks began seaborne trade with them in the 8th century BC and they used the name Philistia for the entire region. Thus, via the Graeco-Roman world, one of the names of the land is still Palestine.

Excavating a naturalistic anthropoid coffin at Deir el-Balah in the Gaza Strip.

The Philistines

Detail from the reliefs at Ramesses III's temple at Medinet Habu showing enemies captured by the Egyptians. Their feather headdresses identify them as Philistines.

The lords of the Philistines went up against Israel. And when the children of Israel heard it, they were afraid of the Philistines. And the children of Israel said to Samuel, Cease not to cry unto the Lord our God for us, that he will save us out of the hand of the Philistines.

1 Samuel 7, 7–8

THE PHILISTINES ARE THE ONLY group of Sea Peoples to be mentioned by name in the Old Testament, presumably because they were such a thorn in the flesh of the nascent Israelite state. The Bible twice mentions that they came from a place called Capthor (Amos 9, 7 and Jeremiah 47, 4), but its identity is the subject of much debate. Most scholars associate Capthor with either Cyprus or Crete; some evidence certainly suggests that the Philistines had a connection with Crete.

Confrontation with Israel

Once the Philistines had established a foothold in the southern part of the Canaanite coast, they organized themselves into at least five major city-states: Ashdod, Ashkelon and Gaza on the coast, and Gath and Ekron inland. By the 11th century BC the next generation of Philistines had begun to expand their territory eastwards into the low, fertile hills of the Shephelah region and northeastwards into Judaea. Here they came into conflict with Israelite tribes who were themselves expanding westwards from the hill country towards the sea (pp. 70–71).

The Old Testament accounts of these struggles are contained in the books of Judges and 1 Samuel. By the time of Saul, *c.* 1020 BC, the Philistines had clearly subjugated at least some of the Israelite tribes. The first book of Samuel (1 Samuel 13, 19–22) tells how the Philistines prevented the Israelites from owning weapons and charged exorbitant rates for sharpening even agricultural tools. Some scholars interpret this to mean that the Philistines had a monopoly on ironworking, which allowed them to dominate the Israelites, who only had bronze arms. But no metal is specified. In fact, in the reliefs of Medinet Habu, the Philistines wield great bronze swords; and iron equipment is not generally not found in common use in the eastern Mediterranean until the 10th century BC. What little has been found is mostly jewellery.

Samson and the tribe of Dan

The original territory of the Israelite tribe of Dan on the western edge of Judaea must have borne the brunt of Philistine expansionism. Joshua (19, 46) tells us that the River Yarkon was the boundary between the tribe of Dan and the Philistines, and it is at just this point (now on the northern outskirts of Tel Aviv) that the Philistine town of Tell Qasileh has been excavated. Founded in the second half of the 12th century BC, the town lies on the Yarkon, not far from the Mediterranean; the river would have provided a convenient route to the sea for maritime trade. Tell Qasileh was devastated by fire in the 10th century BC. The scale of the conflagration was so great that archaeologists think it was destroyed by King David during his military operations to control the Philistines.

The social structure of the Israelites in the early days was based on tribal units. These units rarely joined forces, so resistance to the Philistines tended to be organized by tribe. One of the Danite leaders or Judges was Samson, a charismatic hero about whom many stories are told in Judges 13–16 (see box). He managed to hold the Philistines at bay for 20 years, but when he died his tribe could no longer withstand Philistine pressure and fled far to the north, to the sources of the River Jordan. There they captured the Canaanite town of Laish and resettled it under their own tribal name of Dan (pp. 83–84). It is interesting to note that despite all the hostility between the Israelites and the Philistines, social contacts and even marriages took place between the two peoples.

A king in Israel

Philistine power over Israel increased when the Philistines captured the Ark of the Covenant in the second phase of the Battle of Aphek (1 Samuel 4). It was probably in response to the growing Philistine menace that the Israelite people petitioned Samuel for a permanent leader: 'now make us a king to judge us like all the nations' (1 Samuel 8, 5). Samuel, who was the last and the greatest of the Judges, was bitterly opposed to the idea, because it showed that the people rejected God as their king. But he eventually anointed Saul, of the tribe of Benjamin, to be king, 'a man head and shoulders above his fellows' (1 Samuel 9, 2). Saul was never to be successful in overthrowing the Philistines, indeed his house was all but destroyed at the fatal battle of Gilboa, as related in 1 Samuel 31. However, his successor King David seems to have had little trouble in containing them (pp. 72–74).

The Philistines remained an independent entity along the southern part of the coast until at least the late 8th century BC, when Sargon, King of Assyria, devastated Philistia. Sargon's annals mention in particular the revolt of the Philistine town of Ashdod and its swift submission to his army (Isaiah 20, 1). The Assyrians installed local client kings and they used Philistia throughout the 7th century BC as the springboard for their attacks on Egypt. The Philistines do not quite disappear from history until the Babylonian invasions of the early 6th century BC, which swept away both Judah and Philistia.

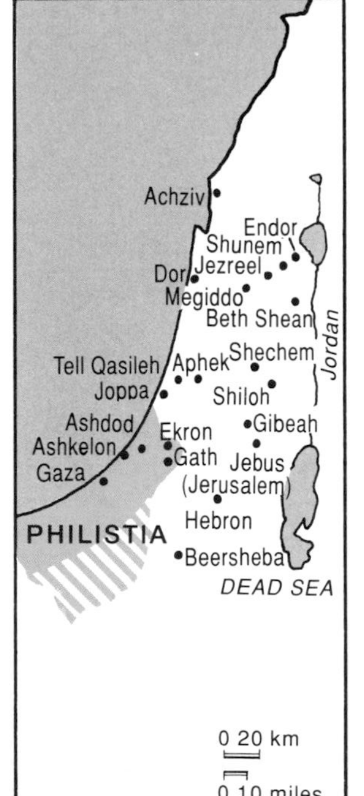

Map showing the area settled by the Philistines and its relationship to the emerging Israelite kingdom.

Philistine art often displays Aegean influence. Found at Ashdod (hence its name, Ashdoda), this female figurine may represent the Mother Goddess in the form of a birthing chair. Some scholars see similarities in her to seated figurines from Mycenae.

SAMSON DEFIES THE PHILISTINES

Samson was born into the tribe of Dan. His impending birth was announced to his mother by an angel, who told her he was to be a Nazirite, that is, dedicated to God all his life. As a symbol of this dedication he was never to drink wine nor to cut his hair, on penalty of losing his God-given strength. This strength and his headstrong nature led him into many adventures and brawls with the Philistines, but he also fell in love with a Philistine girl – Delilah – who cut off his hair while he was asleep. Deprived of his strength, he was at the mercy of the Philistines, who blinded and enslaved him.

At the end of his life the Philistines brought him to their great temple of Dagon. Samson prayed to God to recover his strength just once more. His wish granted, he pushed against the two main supporting pillars of the temple so that the roof caved in, killing him and all his captors.

THE PHOENICIANS AND THEIR NEIGHBOURS

A fine pottery mask of a Phoenician from Achziv, 5 in. (13 cm) high, painted red and black.

This exquisite terracotta figurine was made in a two-part mould and measures just over 9 in. (23 cm) high. It, too, comes from Achziv and dates to the 7th or 6th century BC. *Seated on a chair with a stool at her feet, a woman calmly and thoughtfully awaits the birth of her child. This is the finest example of its type found to date, although many other similar ones are known. Such figurines were perhaps intended to ensure, through sympathetic magic, a successful pregnancy and an easy birth.*

The Phoenicians, to whom Sidon belongs, live in Syria.
Herodotus, *The Histories*, 2, 119

So Saul took the kingdom over Israel, and fought against all his enemies on every side, against Moab, and against the children of Ammon, and against Edom...and against the Philistines: and whither soever he turned himself he vexed them.
I Samuel 14, 47

AS EARLY AS THE 9TH OR 8TH centuries BC the name 'Phoenician' was coined by Greek seaborne traders for the people of the northern coast of the Levant, in approximately the area known today as the Lebanon.

Purple folk

The Greek *phoinikoi* can be translated as 'people of the purple dye'. The dye, one of the rarest and most expensive commodities of the ancient world, was derived from two varieties of the murex sea snail, found along the Levantine coast. The colours produced were red purple ('Tyrian purple') and blue purple (violet or hyacinth), respectively called *argaman* and *tchelet* in the Bible. From then on purple has been symbolic of majesty and wealth.

At the time of the Israelite kingdom, Phoenicia consisted of independent city-states, the most important of which were Sidon, Tyre, Gebal (later Byblos) and Arvad. The Phoenicians would not have called themselves by this collective Greek name, but rather considered themselves as citizens of their individual city-states, which is also how the Bible refers to them.

Phoenician civilization can be defined as a new and brilliant phase of Canaanite culture that developed in the cities of the narrow coastal corridor of Syria and northern Lebanon in the 1st millennium BC. The emergence of the Phoenician cities as independent entities after 1200 BC, the onset of the Iron Age, was connected with the great political and social upheavals at this time (pp. 62–63). With the establishment of the new kingdoms, including Israel (pp. 70–71), controlling inland areas, the Phoenicians relied on international trade for their livelihood.

Historically elusive

The best archaeological information about the Phoenicians comes from sites in northern Israel, along the coast from Mt Carmel to Rosh Hanikrah and in the plain of Acre, for instance Tell Keisan and Achziv. At Achziv a large cemetery has been excavated, containing evidence for two kinds of burial practice: inhumation in rock-cut or stone-built chambers and cremation, with ashes placed in pottery vessels. Cremation is uncommon in the Levant before this time, and may be evidence for the arrival of foreigners from the north.

The great Phoenician cities of the Lebanon are still important urban centres today, making extensive excavation difficult. Tyre has produced evidence for pottery styles which reach back into the Early Bronze Age.

The Phoenicians are credited by the Greeks with the invention, or at least the early development, of the alphabet, which was no doubt of great use in their widespread commercial activities. In the virtual absence of surviving Phoenician literature, much of what is known about the Phoenicians comes from the Bible and other literary sources, such as the royal Assyrian archives, Greek writers, especially the Homeric poems, and contemporary inscriptions. A particularly interesting insight into the growing independence of the Phoenician and other cities is given by the Egyptian account of the temple envoy Wenamon of the late 12th century BC. Sent to Byblos to obtain timber, he found himself being treated with less respect than an Egyptian might formerly have expected in this area. While in the Tjekker city of Dor, supposedly under Egyptian control, he was robbed and then chased by the Tjekker in their fleet of ships to Byblos, where he finally managed to obtain his timber.

Great traders

The Phoenicians are especially famous as great seafarers, travelling long distances in pursuit of trade. They established colonies throughout the Mediterranean, from Kition in Cyprus to southern Spain, and, of course, north Africa, where Carthage (founded, according to one tradition, around 813 BC) was their most famous city. The sites chosen by the Phoenicians were usually natural harbours and promontories, which were then transformed into prosperous ports. The most renowned Phoenician trading partnership was that between Hiram of Tyre and Solomon, to Ophir, to obtain gold, gemstones, exotic woods and strange apes (1 Kings 9, 26–28 and 10, 11; 22). Legend has it that the Phoenicians even sailed beyond the Pillars of Hercules (the Straits of Gibraltar) to Britain to trade in Cornish tin.

Brilliant craftsmen

As well as being the foremost traders of the period, the Phoenicians also excelled as craftsmen. Descendants of the Canaanites, they inherited all the technological skills that had produced such excellent craftsmanship under the Egyptian empire. To the south, in Canaan proper, these skills were no longer much in evidence during the Israelite monarchy; perhaps when the Egyptians withdrew from this area they took with them the finest local craftsmen. David and Solomon both turned to Tyrian craftsmen and artists to build the palaces and the Temple of Jerusalem (pp. 80–81).

Detail of a relief from the palace of Sargon at Khorsabad, showing Phoenician sailors rowing a boat with a prow in the shape of a sea-monster's or horse's head.

The fine stone and timber, including pine and cedar, of their native mountains were used to build homes for gods and kings. The Phoenician artists skilfully combined elements of both Egyptian and Canaanite traditions with inspiration of their own, to produce unrivalled wood carvings, ivory furnishings, gold objects, bronzework and other luxury items, such as jewellery, sealstones and terracottas.

A 19th-century AD illustration of Cedars of Lebanon. Cedars are slow-growing, spreading trees of great beauty. It is one of the few native trees of the Levant which grows to a great height and so could be used for roof and wall beams and planking. Its odour is pleasing to humans but repellant to insects and the wood was thus much used in antiquity in palaces and temples, where it gently perfumed the halls and sanctuaries. The interior of Solomon's Temple in Jerusalem was completely lined with cedar, probably ornately carved (1 Kings 6, 15).

CONTEMPORARIES OF THE PHOENICIANS

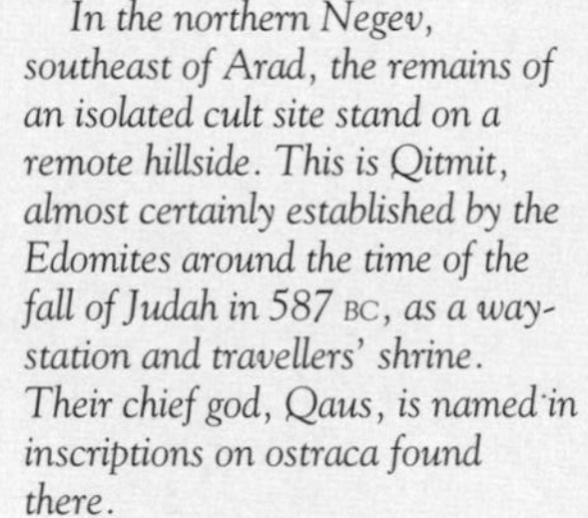

An extraordinary pottery head modelled in the form of a horned goddess (above). This comes from Qitmit, the Edomite cult site, and dates to the 7th or early 6th century BC.

Ammonite limestone sculpture of a bearded male head (left), possibly a god, wearing the Egyptian *atef* crown.

There were many other small nations in the region where King David established his state in the 10th century BC. At that time, as today, great religious and cultural diversity existed in the Near East, especially in the Levant. The rise of such a small nation as Israel to the status of a great power could only have happened when Mesopotamia and Egypt were at a low ebb. As soon as these lands began to recover, nearly all the tiny kingdoms that had gained ground in the interim were again caught up in the power struggle between the resurgent empires. The Bible names many people in the region. Indeed, the prophets frequently warned the Children of Israel against adopting the cultural and religious practices of their neighbours, showing special intolerance towards the Canaanites, who were the indigenous inhabitants of the land.

THE ARAMAEANS

To the north, in Syria, lived the Aramaeans, who were one of the Semitic peoples of the area. They, like the Phoenicians and other Canaanites, were organized in small city-states, chief among them Damascus and Zobah. David conquered some and brought others within his sphere of influence, though after his reign there was seldom peace between them and Israel and Judah.

The Aramaeans controlled the main roads to and from Mesopotamia, Anatolia and Egypt. The Aramaic language was widely used throughout the Near East, supplanting Akkadian, the language of Mesopotamia, as the common tongue of the whole region until well into the Roman period.

THE AMMONITES

More closely related to the Israelites were the peoples of Ammon, Moab and Edom in Transjordan. Until recently little was known about them archaeologically. Conquered by David, they partly broke away from his successors. After the Assyrian conquest of Israel in 721 BC, they became vassals of Assyria, though still controlling both overland trade with Arabia and seaborne commerce on the Red Sea.

The Ammonite capital was at Rabbah (now Amman, the capital of Jordan) 25 miles (40 km) east of the Dead Sea. Some Israelites lived among the Ammonites in the land of Gilead, such as the tribes of Reuben, Gad and half the tribe of Manasseh. David sought refuge among them and Rehoboam, who succeeded his father Solomon, had an Ammonite mother. An inscription from a temple at Tell Deir 'Alla (possibly biblical Succot) tells of a vision of Balaam son of Beor, a prophet (pp. 20–21). The language of the inscription is a dialect of Canaanite, just as Hebrew is, and the script is not dissimilar.

THE MOABITES

Moab, south of Ammon, also had close links with Israel. Ruth, the Moabite girl who twice married Israelites, was the ancestress of King David. The king sent his parents to safety with King Mizpah of Moab when he fled from Saul (1 Samuel 22, 3–4).

One of the greatest kings of Moab was Mesha. He won his country's independence from Israel after the death of Ahab, around 850 BC; an event recorded on the famous Stela of Mesha (p. 28). Again the language and script differ little from Canaanite or Hebrew of the same period.

THE EDOMITES

In the extreme south of Transjordan lived the Edomites, about whom little is known before the Assyrian conquest. They dominated the southern half of the King's Highway and during the 7th century BC they probably took Tell el-Kheleifeh, at the head of the Gulf of Aqaba, from Judah. They thus controlled sea traffic on the Red Sea and the overland routes to Gaza and to Midian, in Arabia, to the southeast.

In the northern Negev, southeast of Arad, the remains of an isolated cult site stand on a remote hillside. This is Qitmit, almost certainly established by the Edomites around the time of the fall of Judah in 587 BC, as a way-station and travellers' shrine. Their chief god, Qaus, is named in inscriptions on ostraca found there.

The Edomites prospered at the expense of Judah after the Babylonian destruction of Jerusalem (pp. 96–97). Some of them migrated west and established the state of Idumaea in southern Judah, where the population had been greatly depleted by warfare and exile.

In addition to these peoples the Bible mentions many others living among and around the people of Judah. Some, such as the Amalekites and Midianites, were nomadic. All of them exercised influence over the culture of the biblical kingdom.